Alexandra Shulman

Clothes...
and other things that matter

 CASSELL

An Hachette UK Company
www.hachette.co.uk

First published in Great Britain in 2020 by Cassell,
an imprint of Octopus Publishing Group Ltd
Carmelite House
50 Victoria Embankment
London EC4Y 0DZ
www.octopusbooks.co.uk

ISBN 978-1-78840-198-2

A CIP catalogue record for this book is available from the
British Library.

Printed and bound in the United Kingdom

10 9 8 7 6 5 4 3 2 1

Publisher: Alison Starling
Creative Director: Jonathan Christie
Editor: Ella Parsons
Copy Editor: Charlotte Cole
Production Controller: Emily Noto
Picture Research Manager: Giulia Hetherington

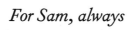

For Sam, always

Contents

Introduction

In winter of 2018 I counted the clothes in my wardrobe. This is what I found:

- 22 coats
- 35 dresses
- 5 full-length evening gowns
- 34 jackets
- 37 skirts
- 17 pairs of trousers
- 16 shirts
- 7 not-immediately-categorizable tops
- 12 cardigans
- 18 sweaters
- 35 T shirts
- 4 sweatshirts
- 3 swimming costumes
- 6 bikinis
- 8 sarongs
- 1 pair of shorts
- 3 track suit tops
- 4 track suit bottoms
- 31 knickers

- 35 bras
- 5 slips
- 5 vests
- 4 pyjamas
- 2 nightdresses
- 24 pairs of tights
- 7 leggings
- 4 dressing gowns
- 21 pairs of socks
- 16 scarves and shawls
- 4 hats
- 9 gloves
- 4 fur tippets
- 6 pairs sneakers or trainers
- 8 pairs long boots
- 3 pairs ankle boots
- 34 pairs heeled shoes
- 24 pairs flats
- 6 pairs slippers
- 37 handbags

I didn't really know what to do with this information once I had it. The tally had been made with no plan in mind. It was more of a diversionary tactic than anything else, in the hope that it would help me work out what this book could be. I knew that I wanted to write, in some way or other, about my life as Editor of *Vogue*, but burdened by a rubbish memory, and having no desire to write an autobiography, I was floundering around. Clothes, I thought perhaps, might be a start.

Since I left university at 23 I had dressed to go to work – and more specifically, most days, to go to an office. That winter was the first since I was a student when I would be spending more time at home. When I wouldn't be driven in my choice of what to wear by my job. By that point I had been out of *Vogue* for about six months and already there was a huge change in how I felt about clothes. Not only did I feel more free in my life, but also in the way I dressed. For the first time in years I was really enjoying my clothes, now that they weren't such an enormous part of my job.

For more than 25 years clothes had been an integral part of my professional life. *Vogue* is foremost a fashion magazine. A place to find inspiration and information about clothes. I had loved working with the very best photographers, stylists and writers. And I adored the activity of putting a magazine together, publishing images and stories I felt were important and chronicling life through the *Vogue* filter. But being surrounded by all those clothes had made them the stuff of work, not of my personal pleasure.

What I found when I went through my cupboards made me think about what those clothes – all clothes – had meant to me. Many of the dresses and skirts were very precious and beautiful. They were like a fine china tea set brought out perhaps twice a year for a special occasion, which demands a laid tray rather than a couple of mugs plonked on the table. Others – knitwear, pencil skirts, dresses, jackets, high heels – I wore to the office but rarely dressed in otherwise. While still others were the clothes that I would put on to slough off *Vogue* – the responsibility, the office politics, the endless continuum of making things happen – when I came home in the evenings or on holiday or on weekends. Contemplating them all, I realized how many things there were that I couldn't imagine having the opportunity to wear again. Or certainly no need for so many. All those navy jackets, the full-length gowns, even the fur tippets.

At the date of the count I was spending much of my time at home, and, it being mid-winter, much of the time in thick sweaters and socks, discovering for myself, as my boyfriend and son had often complained, how cold the house was on weekdays when the heating was off! So many of the clothes on that list were for a different life – of centrally heated offices, of bustling restaurants, of expense-account cars, of red-carpet evenings and of business breakfasts.

As I thought about what to do with the clothes, I became more interested in what the different items had meant to me. About why I had bought them. What I hoped I might feel wearing them. Why some things I had bought again and again. Why we wear the things we wear and why some we keep and get rid of others. Which we attach an emotional value to and why. And what could be said about the world we live in by looking at the clothes we wear.

I may have worked in the fashion industry for many years but my relationship with clothes was established long before that. For most of my life they have mattered hugely to me. Like many children, I cared deeply about the way I was dressed and still remember the joy of the moment when I was allowed to choose my own clothes – a great deal later on than children do now. No more tartan 'trews' as our mother called the sack-like Viyella trousers we were often seen in. No more white socks cutting into my legs. As soon as I could I spent most of my spare time wandering around shops and any cash I had on clothes. I was always excited by a new piece of clothing. How it always did, and now does again, make me feel it is much more than just a piece of cloth. As I see a floral dress, an indigo shirt, a checked coat hanging there I also see the whole, improved life that I am going to live in it. They offer a thrilling potential.

Jason, Dad, Nicky, Mum and me photographed by Aunt Constance in 1969

The more I thought about the book the more I realized how intricately clothes are bound up with our roles. And it is those roles I am interested in just as much as the clothes I have worn when living them: privileged London child, arty teenager, thriving media girl, magazine executive, mother, wife, lover, friend, sister, daughter.

Clothes don't fit into simple timelines and so there are none here. The story jumps around, sometimes dipping back into the history of a garment, sometimes looking at how a specific piece became emblematic of a certain point in time and of my life. There are periods where clothes seem to have been much more important and where my recollection is more vivid. And months, even years, where frankly I have no idea what I wore at any given time.

The pieces I write about have been chosen because they have at some time or other meant something to me. A few are utterly idiosyncratic, others part of many women's collections. Ultimately, though, this book is entirely personal. How much can be traced through the contents of our wardrobes – in my case, 556 pieces? These clothes are the story of my life and my preoccupations; like everyone's, they are unique.

Start-rite shoe advertisement from the Fifties

I.

Red Shoes

Children take their original surroundings for granted. It never occurred to me that the walk from the London flat where we lived to Harrods, where we were taken to buy our school shoes, was anything other than the kind of expedition everybody did. We would cross the big garden squares where we bicycled and played 'ring-a-ring o' roses', and march up the cream stucco streets of Belgravia, home to Greek shipping dynasties and American film producers; they were immaculate and quiet.

The best bit was when we reached Knightsbridge and turned into Hans Place, where we could look into the window of a pet shop in the street, a window that was always filled with treacly-eyed puppies, before reaching the gigantic red brick emporium round the corner. There we would take the ornate gilded cage of a lift, with a uniformed lift boy who handled the brass 'going UP' levers, laconically reciting the content of each floor.

The children's shoe department was not far from the lift, and as we approached you could see the small red chairs where you sat and could twirl around as if on a fairground ride. It was a rewarding activity as we waited for the shoes to be boxed up and payment to be made – another exciting moment involving a pneumatic tube whooshing down to a mystery destination.

Our red shoes were always Start-rite. Their famous logo of two woollen-hatted children seen from behind, as they walked along their straight, tree-lined, golden path to a future, was as familiar to me then as the double C of Chanel and the G of Gucci would become in later life. Even though this logo was designed in the Fifties, their outfits were unisex enough to please the most gender fluid advocate of now. They both wear trousers and the child on the left, in a green all-in-one, is only differentiated from his friend (or more likely sibling) on the right by her hair; she is clearly a girl because, if you look closely, she has plaited hair, while he has a completely bare neck under the hat. At the time I didn't question this, but the way they were dressed looked nothing like anyone I knew – all of us girls wore dresses or skirts and the boys mostly wore shorts with shirts tucked in.

The measuring process for my new shoes was always miserable. Although my feet were of perfectly normal length, the sight of the kneeling shop assistant as they stretched the tape over the sliding measure around the widest part of my foot was always a grim moment. 'I'm afraid...modom,' they would say, 'she's a double E.' The words double E would not in themselves have struck me as so terrible were it not for that loaded 'afraid', followed by a pause that indicated, even to a child, that bad news was on the way.

As time passed, the implications of double E became clear. Rarely were the delicate, pointed-toe styles of our 'indoor' red school shoes available in double E. My best friend, Jane, with her slim feet, had these more stylish versions decorated with sharp diamond cut-outs, while I was stuck with the uglier round-toed version, where the smaller, indeterminate-shape cut-outs lacked the crisp prettiness of hers.

It was obvious that shoes like mine were less glamorous, though I would not have been able to articulate what glamour was. But even at eight years old I knew that it was my broad and indelicate double-E size feet that were barring me from being someone I would have preferred to be.

And so it is that red shoes are almost the only colour shoes that have no place in what has always been my substantial shoe collection. Stamped with these childhood associations, my plodding, bulky feet never had the magical dancing allure that many associate with shoes this colour.

Hans Christian Andersen's story 'The Red Shoes' tells of the vain Karen, who is condemned to dance forever in her own pair, unable to remove them or to still the motion. Her buying them is intended to show her to be wealthy, indulged and frivolous. They lead to her eternal damnation.

It's a harsh positioning of a piece of clothing, but red shoes are undeniably show-off. There is never anything quiet about them. From scarlet to carmine, pillar box to rose, a pair of red shoes have the urgency of the red light, the spark of heat. They will dominate any outfit, attract attention and wordlessly tell those looking at your feet – as people always do when you wear red shoes – that it's here the real story lies.

It's why red shoes have often been a favourite of women who dress soberly for reasons to do with their profession or because it's simply how they feel most comfortable appearing. Teachers, doctors, academics, lawyers – for them the red shoes can announce what the rest of their outfit disguises. That they have another playful, provocative side to them. The filmmakers of *The Wizard of Oz* knew exactly that when they changed the colour of Dorothy's slippers to ruby from silver, so that they would stand out gloriously and memorably on the Yellow Brick Road.

2.

Sloppy Joe

Today I am wearing a loose-knit sweater in a disrupted rainbow of faded colours. When I bought it I had thought it would make me feel nurtured and enveloped in the darkest days of the winter we were then suffering. The muted shades slide from a mottled lemon to a dusty blue and then into a rose. They are soft, gentle colours. The sleeves are overlong, reaching to my fingertips in a burnt umber that merges with a speckled green, and the whole baggy jumper hangs to mid-hip.

I had bought the sweater for myself as a post-Christmas treat, previously considering it as a potential gift for my niece. But when I sent the online link to my sister — her mother — to examine, she replied immediately that she didn't really think it was to my niece's taste, although she could see why I liked it. She thought it was very me. That reminded me of how, when I suggested a song we might play at our father's funeral, she said the same thing. The recherché cover version of Leonard Cohen's 'If It Be Your Will' was very me. Not very him.

Oversized, swampy sweaters should be worn curled up by the fire with a cup of something scented and soothing.

They are not the kind of thing you wear to go out and get things DONE. No, they are the kind of thing you wear to avoid getting on with life and instead spend time, as an example, in a Spotify labyrinth starting with 'Ode to Billie Joe' by Bobbie Gentry that can lead you on to music by Lucinda Williams, Gene Clark and Mercury Rev. As it happens, my favourite version of that Gentry song is by Sinéad O'Connor, who nails her colours to the mast on the pressing question of what it really was that the narrator and Billy Joe threw off the Tallahatchie Bridge. In her recording you hear the brief, small cry of a baby. This is the kind of music that you listen to and the things you think about when you wear these sweaters, a type that used to be called Sloppy Joes. I doubt that anybody wears a Sloppy Joe to listen to the high voltage music of Cardi B or Calvin Harris or Dua Lipa. And in the unlikely event they might, they certainly nowadays wouldn't call it by that name.

The big attraction of oversized knits is that they make us small. In reality they don't, but we imagine they do. They envelop us and yet don't confine or restrict us. They are go-tos for when you wish to disappear, to retract like a snail into your shell. And it's not only teenagers who pull the long sleeves down over their hands for angsty fiddling and feel comforted by the whole garment covering bosoms, bottom, stomach, thighs – all the areas that so many women of all ages question about themselves. Sloppy Joes are deliberately asexual because they disguise the body and are therefore comforting to wear at times when sex is not something you want to have to deal with. Not just when you don't want to have it, such as after eating too much dinner or when a new episode of *Killing Eve* is infinitely more to your taste. But when you don't even want the notion of it to be part of your life.

When I was a teenager I had a much-treasured cream Aran sweater which was bought, like many of my clothes at that time, from Laurence Corner, a well-known army surplus store off the Euston Road. It reached my thighs and I wore it most weekends. The first trip I was allowed to take abroad without adults was to Paris, and I have a photograph of myself, wearing the sweater and a Biba silk scarf, staring over the Seine from the Pont Neuf with my great friend Caroline. The previous week in London, Caroline (and it was she not us because, believe me, she was nymph-style gorgeous) had been picked up when we were hanging around on the Kings Road by some much older guy who had said, over the cup of tea he bought us, that funnily enough he and his friend Alan were going to be in Paris that weekend too. Why didn't they take us out? And we had said, sure.

John, as we learned was his name, telephoned me the evening before we left, to say that he and this friend would be taking us to a restaurant called the Tour d'Argent and since it was smart we should take something smart to wear. Not jeans. I took the call standing in the hall at home where the telephone was and I remember telling my parents about his message and them saying that yes, it was a very smart restaurant. It was famous for its fraises du bois. They did not say, why on earth is some wealthy guy you haven't even met taking you two 17-year-olds out to a wildly expensive restaurant in Paris?

Anyway the Aran was ditched in the Hôtel de Nesle, then a flophouse somewhere off Saint-Germain where we were staying, and we headed out for dinner. Caroline wore a satin Forties-type dress and was regrowing the eyebrows she had shaved off in tribute to David Bowie the previous year, and I wore something stitched together from vintage scarves. At the Tour d'Argent, in a dining room high above the river with vast sparkling chandeliers, painted ceilings and many rococo-style mirrors, we were served their trademark pressed duck – the first duck I had ever tasted and rather terrifying in appearance – and had the fraises du bois for pudding. It emerged that the guy we hadn't met, the one who was paying, was a member of a wealthy retail family in London, and the other, who

First solo trip to Paris wearing my Aran sweater, 1975

was by far the chattier, was it later turned out a kind of procurer for the former, regularly patrolling the Kings Road in search of fresh young flesh. Both had short hair and standard Euro-style blazers, ties and loafers.

They had a chauffeur-driven car and after dinner they suggested we go to Régine's nightclub. I am now and I was then the kind of girl who wears Sloppy Joes and not the kind of girl who feels at all at home in a famously hedonistic Parisian nightclub. Let alone in the company of strangers who were at least a decade older and clearly wanting only one thing. I tried to say no, that it was very kind of them but it was time we headed back to the hotel. But Caroline, who was then and no doubt still is exactly the kind of girl who was at home in any nightclub anywhere in the world, was having none of it. She was raring to go.

So we went – speeding along the riverside Quai to the club, with its disco lights and dancefloor and a table that had been set aside for us. Caroline was straight onto the floor. She was a brilliant dancer. Tall and slender with a liquid-gold bob, her large mouth painted crimson, singing as she undulated. The men watched as she performed entirely for herself, not, as they thought, for them. But I was miserable. Unwilling to dance near this vision of pulchritude, I was left with the option of sitting with the two guys, arms snaking closer to me across the back of the banquette as they ogled Caroline, knowing that at some point, in an hour or maybe two, but at some stage, sure as eggs were eggs, the payback moment would come. I was a virgin and this was not the way I intended to change that condition, indulging in some creepy sex with unattractive older guys we were never going to have anything to do with again. When there was a short break in the disco relay of 'Jive Talking', 'Love To Love You Baby' and Gloria Gaynor's 'Never Can Say Goodbye' – all the hits of the time – I dragged an objecting Caroline off, shouting to our hosts that we were leaving. John was furious, as I recall. Did they let us use the chauffeur? Don't remember that.

Many years later, I was going to the couture shows in Paris and as the Eurostar train pulled up at the Gare du Nord a man approached me and introduced himself. It was John. He offered to help with my cases, and when we were on the platform I asked him how he could have behaved the way he did all those years back? He gave a strange noncommittal smile, didn't reply and walked away with a light shrug.

This was many years before the explosion of women's outrage that created #MeToo and Time's Up, when women in every profession came forward, one after the other, with tales of sexual harassment, of casting couch negotiations, of inappropriate abuse of power. When men in all walks of life were accused of making unwanted sexual approaches. When, if you are a woman of my generation, you can find yourself conflicted in your reactions to all of this.

So many of us have been felt up or propositioned or had to navigate clumsy not-safe-in-taxi passes which we accepted as part and parcel of our existence. Should we retrospectively be analysing our reactions to that? Were we wrong to think that usually they were an embarrassing bore, although occasionally they could veer into the much more difficult dark side of being wanted and desirable, which were, let's face it, what most of us sought to be? The friend of a friend's parent who fondled my breasts late at night on a summer holiday, the Rasta DJ who stalked me day and night outside my flat, the cherished older male mentor who one night lunged as he dropped me home. And the terrifying, creepy paedophilia of a Jeffrey Epstein who could, incidentally, so easily have been our date at the Tour d'Argent.

Viewed through today's lens the episode in Paris was at best sordid, but at that time it didn't occur to us that it was wrong to be expected to take part in a sexual transaction, for that was surely what it would have been. We had imagined that we could handle the trade-off of the possibility (not, mind you, the actuality) of sex with a couple of schoolgirls for an evening of true jet-set living. As it happened, Caroline could. But when it came down to it, jammed into a plush booth late at night in a foreign city with these predatory guys, all I yearned for was to be back at home with a half of lager and lime in some Hammersmith pub and wearing something utterly unglamorous and asexual like my Sloppy Joe. Something that was safely off-putting, if a voluptuous babe was what you were after one night.

A few years later, I knitted a Sloppy Joe on large needles. It was no more than four pale green wool rectangles, stitched together to make a sweater. The neck was a totally straight line and the sleeves were huge wide things. So really not very nice as such. It was perfect though for my first term at university where everyone was wearing homespun-looking clothes and drank out of brown pottery mugs and tried to grow grass on their bedroom window ledges in the university halls.

I was allocated Andrew, a sponsor from the year above, to look after me. He had an earring and cropped black hair, and we drank endless cups of tea in the corridor kitchen. Andrew came from further up north than I had ever visited in my narrow south-eastern life and was gently mocking of my voice and ways. I have often wondered what shape his life has taken. When he saw me in that Sloppy Joe, which I wore most days, he said his aunt had knitted one just like that. But she only had one arm. I have never known whether that was true or not.

3.

The Bra

There's a point in most women's lives when shopping for bras is consigned to one of those special places in hell. Not, I imagine, the same spot as Donald Tusk had in mind for Brexiteers who had no plan of how to leave the EU, nor the same place that Madeleine Albright suggested women who didn't help other women should end up. But, all the same, an unpleasant destination.

Shopping for bras is not of course the same as buying them. Buying is simply a monetary transaction. Shopping is a whole other ball game. It involves finding the right bra among the millions of options out there: balcony, minimizer, T shirt, bralet, strapless, padded, underwired, push-up. And at some point it is going to involve stripping down, trying it on and exposing your body to self-scrutiny.

A word here before I go further. I did once have nice breasts. On one level they were my best physical asset. They pleased me. So the wearing, or not, of bras has always been something I have given thought to.

Buying your first bra is a rite of passage. It's a material manifestation of the dramatic changes that are happening to your body – underarm and pubic hair appear, pimples and spots suddenly sprout, the new smells, often not entirely pleasant, of humanity replace the sweet scent of childhood. But into this gloomy landscape come bras. They are an exciting addition to life. The first bra is an indication that there will come a time, even if it hasn't come soon enough, when you will be liberated from the many indignities of early adolescence: having to talk to your parents, having your bedtime monitored, having to eat what you are given, having your friends scrutinized. And being told things. All the time. Told what to do, what to say, how you should think. 'If I've told you once I've told you a thousand times.' That's what parents say. And what (memo to those of you not yet initiated) to your horror you too will find yourself saying if you become one.

So a bra is that piece of clothing that shows you are on track to the future. To becoming a woman. Personally, though, I had always wanted to keep absolutely everything about becoming a woman completely private. I had no desire for a public announcement when my first period arrived – actually, I had no idea on earth what was happening. We weren't a family who discussed bodily functions of any kind. I hadn't heard of such a thing. It was terrifying. As I sat on the loo I thought I had some kind of catastrophic bowel condition and couldn't decide how to alert my mother to the ghastliness of what had occurred. If anything, the emergence of my breasts, although not quite as traumatic, was also a matter of extreme embarrassment.

But all the same, owning a bra was a bit of a status symbol, and I was the first to get one among my friends, all of whom were still wearing vests. Nobody actually said that they were wildly jealous of my having breasts. But since we did all want to be grown up, it followed that wearing a bra was some compensation for the acute discomfort I felt at my body changing when no one else's seemed to be.

Bras didn't always carry sexy or glamorous conn-otations. The early versions of what might be considered bras began their existence as hygienic items to prevent the grubby business of skin contaminating clothes. They weren't supporting of breasts but suppressors. For centuries, stiff bodices held bosoms in place to ensure no visible movement, which was another way of saying that they should be hidden. The nearest thing to our notion of a bra was a cloth binding that would also add warmth.

You could argue that change came with the acceptance and admiration of cleavage, which propelled the bra into today's widespread item of underwear. Cleavage, which so clearly defines the breasts as two separate objects, had little public exposure until well into the 20th century. Sculptures

John Singer Sargent's Madame X, *1883–4*

and paintings of women throughout history would often feature bare breasts but they were always portrayed high on the torso, relatively small and self-contained. They never intruded sloppily and droopily outside their own zone. When the breast appeared covered, in clothes or drapery, there was usually no hint of cleavage.

Even by the mid-1800s, when artists like Winterhalter were painting formal portraits of the women society was supposed to admire, such as Queen Victoria and Empress Eugénie, they were given magnificent bare shoulders but the neckline of their gown was always draped over a monobreast. One of the many controversial aspects of Sargent's *Madame X* – his portrait of the French banker's wife Virginie Gautreau – must have been the daring way that the deep black V of the gown, suspended on the slimmest straps, plunged between her white breasts. But even then – no cleavage. It took several decades and a world war for bras that divided the breasts, pushed them up, squished them in, padded them out, to become a big business.

At the time I was getting my first bra – 1969 – bras were of course becoming the symbol of a very different kind of liberation to my longed-for escape from childhood. Not the actual bras, but getting rid of them. A new wave of feminism rejected the bra as a hated symbol of the tyranny of the male gaze. It wasn't regarded as a woman's aide in the creation of a desirable figure, but an accomplice in the denial of all that women naturally were, moulding them into the shape men wanted them to be. In her famous polemic *The Female Eunuch*, Germaine Greer urged the sisterhood to 'refuse to wear undergarments which perpetuate the fantasy of pneumatic boobs, so that men must come to terms with the varieties of the real thing'.

The notorious bra burning, so often referred to as a moment in women's liberation, never happened in reality – instead, a young woman protesting a 1968 Miss America pageant tossed her bra into a 'Freedom Trash Can'. But by the end of the Sixties young women who regarded themselves as cool, intelligent and questioning were rethinking their attitudes to bras. Why were we wearing them? They were restrictive, and often uncomfortable. Whose idealized shape were they moulding us into?

It is, though, wrong to suggest that women do not derive their own pleasure from bras. Not so much from their shape-altering properties but from the way the fabric can feel on your skin, the secret deliciousness of this layer between your body and what the world can see. There is something delightful about knowing your underwear is an object of beauty only revealed to yourself and who you choose. There are countless examples, including that of my friend Marie Colvin, the brave *Sunday Times* foreign correspondent slaughtered in Syria, who would take sustenance and pleasure from wearing something delicate and beautiful under their clothes, no matter how brutal a world their work can take them into.

But this wasn't how I felt at 17, when I stopped wearing a bra and didn't start again until after my son was born 20 years later. It wasn't anything to do with lofty feminist ideals but simply that I hated how they felt; the straps that weighed on my shoulders, the clasp at the back. And I liked the fact that my breasts were just there – a scrap of fabric away from nudity rather than encased in a protective cage.

The only downside was the unavoidable issue of nipples. While I wasn't bothered by it being obvious I wasn't wearing a bra, even so I was less comfortable with the attention-seeking way my nipples would pop up. Inconveniently, this would often be at a time when I particularly didn't want it to happen – say, the morning conference when I was Women's Page editor on the *Sunday Telegraph*, in a room full of male journalists pitching news stories like Gorbachev's new world order or the horror of the *Piper Alpha* oil rig disaster. It was mortifying enough having to announce that the Women's Page contribution to the news of the day was a piece on finding the perfect white T shirt without the realization that one's erect nipples were attracting a certain amount of covert attention.

Fast forward 30 years and I am now the owner of 35 bras, a fact I find hard to believe, especially since I don't love a single one of them. There is a cyclamen cotton scrap and two white lace numbers. Ten black bras in ever-diminishing skimpiness and a beautiful crimson velvet pair of triangles which is really only there for me to look at, rather than wear, since it scarcely contains even half of one of my breasts. They lie in chaotic piles – purple and turquoise, flesh and chocolate, navy and emerald – but none of them manage to do what I want them to do, which is to give me back the breasts I had in those braless times.

That won't happen, I know, but nonetheless with each new bra I hope. I try to find slivers of satin straps rather than things that look like a tree surgeon's pulley. I want a slim band at the back and cups where my breasts are balanced rather than cups that reach nearly to my collarbone. When was it that I became a person who emerged from the M&S changing room, as I did recently, with four bras substantial enough to house a children's tea party? When, in a panic because I was miserable seeing a rash of skin tags on my torso, a bulge of back fat and the disconcerting way my breast seems to have spread to my underarm in the grim changing room mirrors, I bought all of them one size too large.

But that's what it's like in this particular corner of hell. You lose any sense of perspective about your own body and how it has been fortunately healthy, has breastfed a child, is desired by your partner, transports you around. You forget to be thankful for these and many other physical aspects of being that so many people aren't lucky enough to have. You don't appreciate the very real miracle of the fact that you are alive and instead indulge in a maelstrom of self-flagellation and doubt, triggered by an overly judgemental view of what your boobs look like in your bra.

Blue-and-white tea dress from a jumble sale, 1973

4.

Rags and Feathers

The house near Paddington station belonged to a diplomat who was usually posted abroad, while his children went to schools in London. And it was there, in the small, low-ceilinged sitting room, on a Saturday afternoon in 1973, that I first heard Leonard Cohen's 'Suzanne'.

That afternoon, I recall it being late spring but then again it could have been early autumn, we were at a tea party. Lucy, the diplomat's daughter, was three years above me at school and she held weekly tea parties. They seemed, at the time, ineffably glamorous. It was one of the places that we all wanted to hang out. For a start there were always boys there, and since I was at a single-sex school boys were not that easily come by. The boys who came for tea were all in love with Lucy. Not because she was particularly beautiful but because she was like Suzanne. Wearing long skirts and silky scarves, she dished out advice and opinion in a sage, quasi-maternal style.

I was 16, and Suzanne (and for a few months Lucy) were my heroines. Although Cohen wrote the poem that would become one of his most famous songs in 1967, Suzanne was perfectly dressed for this moment, wearing 'rags and feathers' which she bought from the Salvation Army, a style which had launched in the Sixties and which by this point had reached a pinnacle of popularity. Rags and feathers, satin and tat – scavenger style. Who wouldn't want to look like Suzanne, to live like Suzanne by the river? You know, as Cohen sings, that she is unique and wild and forging her own, compelling path. And I knew – and if you are 16 this counts for a great deal – that she was one of my kind because of the way she dressed.

Rags and feathers are sensuous and flowing, they are mobile, unanchored and so different from the confines of a shirtwaister dress, a jacket or a chic shift. They are a world away from the utility of denim or combat, or the bland professionalism of plain black trousers. They are indeterminate of hues, sometimes glittering with the iridescence and splendour of a peacock flashing emerald, turquoise and gold, or possibly muted, as I imagine they are on Suzanne, as she lives her life as a member of the watery community among the driftwood and the mudflats.

My generation of London schoolgirls spent our weekends delving through piles of clothes in church jumble sales or rummaging around the rails of Oxfam and Christian Aid shops. We didn't call the clothes vintage then. And it was years before the Brooklyn hipster concept of thrifting. But we would scour the piles of smelly Terylene and polyester shirts and old men's pyjamas to snuffle out the very rare find of perhaps a peach-coloured silk blouse or a printed Forties tea dress. On the rare occasion that we had enough money we might visit Kensington Market, where there were a few stalls that sold second-hand clothes among the patchouli and sandalwood-scented Indian stuff. Or for the wealthy girls who lived around Chelsea there was Antiquarius which sold proper 'antique' clothing – expensive and collectable.

Suzanne's style has stayed with us – or certainly with me – for more than 50 years. Because when dressed like Suzanne, we can, albeit temporarily, imagine that we too are free spirits, unhampered by mundane realities – emails, mortgages, PowerPoint, Facebook. Most of these didn't exist when Suzanne came into the world, but we know that if they had she would somehow have escaped them. She wouldn't have had to battle with the local visitor-parking system, or so I anyway choose to believe.

No wonder that rags and feathers have become the regulation holiday look, found as the sun sets and the mojitos are mixed on the beaches of Ibiza or Tulum or Costa Rica. You can see it worn by the itinerant travelling population who move between holiday meccas with their dyed braids, piercings, leather sandals and loose trousers, but also by the hedge-fund wives stepping off the yacht. It's there in the long dresses that trail in the sand, their hems dipped in saltwater; dresses which simultaneously hide and reveal with low plunging necks, floating bell sleeves and almost always in light, sheer fabrics. It's there in the feathers of totemic jewellery found in the weekly hippie markets from Goa to Formentera. And it's there, of course, in the style and music of repeating generations of female singers – songwriters from the whirling, bewitching Stevie Nicks through to the flowing robes and revelatory vocals of Florence Welch.

Suzanne is now identified as Suzanne Verdal. She was a beautiful girl who hung out with the jazz musicians of Montreal. When she broke up with her husband, a friend of Cohen's, she moved to an old apartment on the city's St Lawrence River. For a time she would meet Cohen and feed him tea and mandarin oranges. Asked about her rags and feathers, in a 1998 interview, she described herself as an early pioneer of recycling, making herself and her daughters clothes out of old pieces found in charity shops.

Hand-me-downs were not regarded as in any way aspirational until relatively recently, and even now the notion of vintage being desirable has little currency in societies that have been oppressed and deprived for years. The idea that there is exceptional worth in wearing second hand is still baffling to communities who have had nothing else for decades. It's been the privilege of Western cultures who have enjoyed a lengthy period of relative peace and stability to indulge in the luxury of admiring used clothes. Until now.

Under-resourced societies have always recycled through necessity. But not us, who have seen ever-increasing consumerism and the possibility of owning more new stuff as a measure of progress. To make more, to buy more, was after all one of the great by-products of the Industrial Revolution, which transformed the world we lived in. A world in which, after two world wars, our wellbeing as a society became measured by how much we could possess. The sight of the huge skirts of Dior's New Look in 1947 weren't just gorgeous fashion. In their extravagant use of fabric they represented the start of a new order, where clothing rations were no longer dominant, where an indulgent femininity could be celebrated after the austerity of the war years.

Now we know that this culture of possession has a cost. And the expansion of fast fashion over the past few decades is taking a hefty toll on the finite resources of the planet. We've learned of the environmental and ecological damage caused in the production of new clothes – from the abusive employment conditions in sweatshops to the toll on our natural resources of the manufacturing and distribution, the purchasing and the disposal. Recycling has become a growing part of individual and corporate social conscience.

Suzanne Verdal may have thought of herself as a recycler all those years back, but our look was driven by our economics – i.e. having very little cash to spend – and fashion's embrace of the raggle-taggle gypsy. Although we liked our ramshackle appearance and had no desire to be seen in the designer clothes of the time (if indeed we knew what those were), there was no Primark or Zara, H&M or ASOS, so our style depended hugely on army surplus and charity stores. But we didn't, for a second, think that we were doing the planet any good by buying second hand. We had never heard of recycling.

Now the circle is complete. The Duchess of Cambridge is praised for dressing her children in hand-me-downs and repurposing her own clothes. High street chains have recycling initiatives, rental fashion is becoming a growing business and luxury brands see building sustainability into the core of their practices as both essential and a vital marketing tool. Any start-up in fashion has to look at how they can produce clothes that we want to buy as well as clothes that we will feel good about buying. Or at least not feel bad about buying.

The other day a package arrived for me. Inside the brown paper wrapping was a denim jacket with faded paisley-printed cotton inserts on the back and sleeves and in a stripe down the front. Tiny metal shells and starfish hung from a beaded trim. The label stitched into the collar was Shake the Tree. Upcycled from Kenya. It was sent to me by my friend Rachel, a woman who has spent 15 years in the Far East working at the heart of fast fashion, for companies such as Next and New Look and Marks & Spencer. She had returned recently to London with a passion to do it differently, and the jacket was an early excursion into this new world. In her dreams, one of those huge buildings on London's Oxford Street which sell the clothes she used to design would instead be a superstore dedicated to ethical fashion.

The jacket looked like something I might have worn all those years back, wandering around the stalls in Kensington Market in loon pants and a button-down granddad vest, with a fiver nicked from my dad's trousers in my bag, puffing on a menthol Consulate. I wore it yesterday to go to the local farmers' market where children called Casper are encouraged by their stubble-faced Sunday morning fathers to consider stuffed courgette flowers for lunch and to sample the wok-fried gyoza vegetarian dumplings. I bought bags of tomatoes, organic chicken, some slightly wilting parrot tulips, early asparagus and bunches of mint and parsley.

Wheeling my trolley home in the spring sunshine, the seashells tinkling on my back, I wondered what that earlier-version Alexandra would have thought of me now, with my mortgage, my health insurance, my VW Golf and my worries about my pension. I doubt that she would have been impressed. But at least she would have recognized the jacket.

5.

Suits

When I was a child I would visit my American aunt, Constance, at the Berkeley Hotel in Knightsbridge. She was one of the most successful female public relations executives in Los Angeles, and the Berkeley was her home away from home when she travelled to London for corporate clients like IBM and the oil company Exxon. Arriving in the lobby, with its imposing concierge desk and uniformed staff, was always a moment of great excitement. 'I've come to see Constance Stone,' I would say nervously, intimidated by the surroundings, and they would pick up the phone, dial her room and eventually, after what was sometimes a nerve-racking wait, look back with a smile and say, 'She says "Go right on up."'

Constance was the first businesswoman I knew and she made her work look tremendously exciting. She held dinners in what were then the most enjoyable places in London – places like Mr Chow and San Lorenzo – and she would order her favourite drink, a vodka gimlet 'with Rose's lime juice', and bottles of white Italian Gavi di Gavi. She loved to mix us family with her professional life, which often included producers, directors and actors from the

TV world, since her clients sponsored the US runs of many extravagant series, such as the hugely successful *Brideshead Revisited*.

She always wore the same things: suits, in different colours – pink, navy, pale blue, beige – with long jackets and skirts hemmed just above the knee that made the best of her skinny legs, with their nude tights and very high-heeled court shoes. She circled her eyes with thick black eyeliner and from time to time would swipe a pink lipstick briskly along her long thin mouth. Hanging from her neck would be a variety of long chains, often including a small, dangling, magnifying glass. She always had the same room at the Berkeley, where there would be a cheese platter and magazines on the coffee table. When any of us arrived we would invariably find her with the telephone hooked under her chin, scribbling notes on the hotel notepad and waving at us to munch on the cheese and crackers.

The contents of her at least two enormous suitcases and the shopping she would already have done (usually from Harrods) would be spread around the suite. She was the woman who taught me there was no point in capsule packing – if you are checking in anything, why not take everything you might conceivably need? She never took a suitcase with her that didn't need somebody to sit heavily on it to close. And on every visit she would take me shopping.

My first suit – a pale grey Cerruti number with a fine pale blue stripe – was one of her gifts. It was a real treasure. Like Constance's own suits, it had a long jacket with slightly padded shoulders – quite masculine in design – and a straight skirt. It was the most expensive item of clothing I had ever possessed, but, Constance argued, somebody who was now a working girl, having to make an impression in meetings and offices, needed something other than the Portobello Road ragbag I was usually dressed in.

I wore that suit to every important office event and job interview throughout my 20s. I even bought myself a pair of nude, high-heeled courts from Dolcis to go with it. When I wore it I felt exactly the way you were meant to feel in business suits – confident, smart, empowered. The suit was completely different to anything else in my wardrobe, but instead of being an interloper it was an encouragement and support. Because it had been bought for me by Constance.

The timing was perfect. This was the early Eighties and I had just become the features editor of *Tatler* magazine, which I'd joined two years previously (before I was given that suit) after pitching an idea to the then Editor Tina Brown on how Notting Hill was the new fashionable place to live. Bear with me…that was 1983 and not everybody knew that, I promise. As the assistant my main job was writing small captions to go with the Bystander Page parties under the tutorship of Miles Chapman, a clever, demanding man. It was Miles who taught me that no matter how few words you were writing they had to tell a story and not just dull facts. To this day I think that the ability to write 50 words about a party in a house in Oxfordshire where there may or may not have been a marquee and somebody may or may not have got off with someone else, and make it sound even marginally interesting, was a useful life skill.

A couple of years later the brilliant caricaturist and magazine editor Mark Boxer became Editor of *Tatler*. He had known me from when I was younger, and he had no desire to see the person he had considered a somewhat dull and blobby 18-year-old on his SWAT team. I spent a great deal of time in the loo in tears. Mark had a master's degree in mockery and humiliation, but despite his constantly suggesting that I leave and find another job I was determined not to be pushed out.

One afternoon there was a features ideas meeting and somebody suggested that we should try and interview a notorious polo-playing playboy called Luis Basualdo. Basualdo had never done an interview and, anyway, nobody knew where he was. It could have been Chelsea or it could have been Buenos Aires. It could have been

Skorpios, the Onassis island (he was married to Christina Onassis), or Byblos Beach in St Tropez. Mark thought it was a hoot to ask me to do the piece as he fully expected it would be impossible and failure might propel me to finally shuffle off the masthead.

But somehow I found Basualdo and did the interview, which was published under the title of 'The Bounder', and Mark loved it. That article changed my life. From that moment I was my Editor's golden girl. I was given many of the most interesting interviews, often in a low-grade honeytrap way: the rakish Lord Lambton (where I wrote that he enjoyed putting live budgerigars in his gun boots), the amorous academic Norman Stone, who specialized in Eastern Europe and considerable quantities of wine, the blond adman of the moment John Hegarty. None, I might say, ever made a pass at me. Perhaps it was the suit. The closest I ever got to anything approaching such behaviour was being invited on a date with Paul Simon, who I interviewed in his room in the Savoy when *Graceland* was released. He took me to see a play at the Royal Court theatre, but the evening concluded entirely chastely, eating steamed rice at the Groucho Club.

At this point there was a huge expansion of media in Britain – more newspapers, more weekend colour supplements, breakfast TV, Channel 4. In the US, cable

TV was born, and there were new high-profile, female media stars – Oprah Winfrey, Barbara Walters, Tina Brown. Young women became the must-haves for every staff, not because the predominantly male employers really wanted us but because it was thought that hiring us was the right thing to do to appear in tune with the era.

Opportunities flung themselves at my media generation. And we all wore suits from time to time – some most of the time. Often the jackets were tightly buttoned so that it didn't matter what we wore underneath, if anything. Sometimes it might be a body, that leotard-like piece of clothing that was intended to make us more efficient and streamlined, though that was negated by the endless fiddling with the poppers at the crotch every time we went to the loo.

Suits were as much part of our lives as the zippy little Fiat Unos we drove, the fashionable wine bars where you would share a bottle or two with a girlfriend, Pepto-Bismol coloured taramasalata from the 24-hour 7/11, and Margaret Thatcher. If you were in your 20s, well educated and free from domestic responsibility, you could breeze into this world in your Joseph suit and your black opaques with a sense that if you played the right cards it was all there for the taking.

But before us, if we chose to look, were the older women in the office, who had to get home with the carrier bags of shopping they kept under the desk, whispering conversations to their children on the office phone. Women who were still wearing below-the-knee skirts and floral blouses and who we thought we would have such different lives from. But, of course, in the end, have not.

The power dressing of the time played on the idea that clothing for women which mimicked the garb of men would help the climb up the professional ladder. But although Margaret Thatcher had become the first female British Prime Minister, real life power-dressing role models were relatively few. Flicking though the mental Rolodex of women of the age, it's far easier to come up with Madonna in her early bleached pop siren days, Joan Collins in *Dynasty* or Diana, Princess of Wales, than an Angela Merkel or Christine Lagarde. Yet while there may have been few high-profile female leaders to emulate in style terms, fashion was ahead of the game and moving women towards that boardroom table faster than it was happening in reality: tailored trousers, mannish shirts, sharp-shouldered jackets and, naturally, endless suits.

The initial early adopters of this fashion were not in fact employed at anything but were wives of powerful men. Nancy Reagan, Ivana Trump, Nan Kempner, Mercedes Bass – the type of women immortalized in Tom Wolfe's *The Bonfire of the Vanities*. They were the ones who could afford to wear the newly revitalized Chanel with Karl Lagerfeld at its head – boucle tweed suits, pearls, huge gilt buttons, a shoulder that could get you through the door. Their power was their husband's bank balance.

As is often the case, fashion was propelled by the wealthy, who had the time and funds to play around with new ideas, the mainstream following on. These women's husbands were happy to bankroll their frequently second wives' wardrobes, filling them with a glitzy version of power dress, which included the return to mini skirts. We – the 20-something new guard of professionals – regarded them in a different light. All the long lengths flapping around your calves were for yesterday's women; we were going to stride forth with our legs on display. Legs that were taking us places.

It's a curious idea that because you are matching your jacket to your bottom half you are in some way more efficient, but it's an idea that had tremendous traction then and still retains some today. The suit may have lost some of its totemic quality as dress-down culture infiltrates the world of finance and dominates the new age of tech. And when a smart dress and jacket has become an alternative uniform for many women in the public eye. But still the idea that suits convey competence persists – air hostesses, restaurant receptionists, bank tellers, all continue to dress in two pieces of one kind or another, although usually without allowing any of the individual style or identity which can be a mark of real power.

I never felt the same way about any other suit as I did about that first Cerruti suit; about any other suit in my life. Without the emotional association of Constance, what had felt glamorous and luxurious and smart felt hard and corporate and unattractive, and not the way I really wanted to come across.

Extract from my diary, January 1992:

Vogue started on Thursday, January 23rd. That's when I was formally offered the job. I wore a zipped jacket and skirt suit by Lolita Lempicka which my sister Nicky came with me to buy in Browns in South Molton Street. I had new shoes and proper make-up... The night before I felt dreadful waiting for something I didn't necessarily want to happen.

There are pictures of me wearing that black suit in all the interviews I did in the next couple of days, after being anointed Editor. It was the only item of clothing I had that looked anything like how I thought the Editor of *Vogue* should look. The fabric had a little stretch, and the jacket had slightly padded shoulders and a curved silver zip, like a scimitar, that ran across my breast. The cuffs also had zips running up from the wrists. It was a combat outfit.

One of those newspaper articles included a quote from my old headmistress. 'She wasn't particularly academic but she has always had staying power. Perseverance is the greatest quality necessary for success.' That somewhat damning-with-faint-praise observation was followed by a comment from me: 'I've never been a suit person and I'm keen to hold out against a uniform.'

Looking back on this I see a number of inconsistencies. I obviously did feel the need to adopt a uniform as I took over *Vogue*, because what did I do but rush out and buy a suit? My headmistress would have been right about staying power since I remained at *Vogue* for 25 years, but during my school days neither staying power nor perseverance was a notable feature of my school reports. I bought the suit not for an interview for the job but for the day I was to be formally told I had won it. I was in a room faced with a panel of three men. Also in suits. That morning I could have worn anything, I had already got the role, but I needed something to carry me from one life to another and I chose a suit.

I only bought three more suits in my entire time at *Vogue*. And I haven't bought one since.

From men's magazine to editor of Vogue

By Kathryn Samuel
Fashion Editor

ALEXANDRA Shulman, 34, editor of GQ, the men's lifestyle magazine, was appointed editor of British Vogue yesterday, ending a fortnight of speculation over who would succeed Liz Tilberis, who has gone to Harper's Bazaar in the United States.

Shulman was always considered a possibility. In two years she has boosted the circulation of GQ by over 30 per cent to 79,560.

After graduating in social anthropology at Sussex University 13 years ago, she worked as a secretary for two recording companies and then for Over 21 magazine. But in the 10 years since her first journalistic job at Tatler her rise has been swift. In 1987 she became first women's editor, then deputy editor of 7 Days magazine on the Sunday Telegraph, returning to Condé Nast as features editor of Vogue in December 1988.

"Vogue is almost in her blood," said Mr Nicholas Coleridge, Vogue's Managing Director, referring to the fact that her mother Drusilla Beyfus, was an associate editor of Vogue in the '70s, her father Milton Shulman, the writer and theatre critic, was once Vogue's film critic and her brother Jason is currently art editor of Tatler.

Dame Heather Brigstocke, who was Miss Shulman's headmistress at St Paul's School for Girls, said: "She wasn't particularly academic but she has always had staying power. Perseverance is the greatest quality necessary for success."

On the subject of her own style, Miss Shulman said yesterday: "I've never been a suit person and I'm keen to kill out against a uniform. However, I shall be going shopping tomorrow."

Style smile: Alexandra Shulman, the newly-appointed editor of British Vogue

A newspaper cutting published in the Daily Telegraph *the day after I became Editor of British* Vogue, *January 1992*

6.

Hats

She was well known around the bars.
She was known, mostly, for that look of hers —
nothing you could really point to —
that put you in your place. It'd flare up,
kind of sudden, and there you'd be,
wondering what you'd said. No guy thinks
that he can take too much of that,
but I can tell you, there were plenty.
Most of them she wouldn't give the time of day.
A hat? Oh sure, she wore a hat.

FROM 'CONFIDENCE' BY ALAN JENKINS

I met the poet Alan Jenkins at a party in 1983 where, incidentally, many people wore hats. It was a summer lunch party in a London garden. This being the Eighties, when themed parties and clubs were popular, the hostess had decreed her party to be a celebration of the Impressionists. She wore a white, lace-trimmed nightdress tied with a red ribbon sash with a thin black choker tied around her neck, while many of the men were in the pale jackets, white shirts and straw hats of paintings from that period. We sat on the grass and at pretty ironwork tables, a group of young people at the start of their careers, drinking cheap wine in the afternoon sun and into the evening. Whenever the subject of hats arises, I hear the last line of that poem in my head, thumping a Pavlovian tattoo. 'A hat? [beat, beat] Oh sure, she wore [beat, beat] a hat' on repeat.

It sums up the women I have come across who wear hats as a trademark, an addendum to their personality, an extension of their body. They wear them in all weathers, indoors and out. You can spot them, sometimes with a sinking heart, from a distance, weaving their way towards you, determined to be noticed, which they usually are. Because that's what hats do. Perched on the top of a body, hats are robust things. There's nothing mousy about wearing a hat. Sure, they protect the head. But, more importantly, they will make you stand out from the crowd. (Conversely, at formal occasions such as weddings or christenings or as part of uniforms, they achieve the total opposite effect. Then they identify you as a member of a particular group.)

I very rarely wear hats. There is something about the way they draw attention to the face that makes me feel as if I am showing off. All the same, I have a beige wool Afghan pakol which I bought from a stall on Portobello Road and which I wedge on in the cold. And a year ago, in Kiev, when my siblings and I were visiting to see if we could learn anything about our paternal grandmother's roots, I was given a pale brown cap by Ukrainian designer Ruslan Baginskiy, which I am fond of and sometimes use instead of an umbrella.

Despite my ambivalence about hat wearing, hats have a place in our family history. Our grandmother Ethel was born in 1891 in the city of Zhytomyr, 87 miles west of Kiev. It is now in Ukraine but then was a part of Russia. Ethel's family, the Raisbergs, like many other Jewish families threatened by growing anti-Semitism, left their home to make the 4,692-mile journey from the Black Sea to Toronto. It was there she met and married my grandfather Samuel Shulman, also a Russian Jewish immigrant, whose family had made a similar journey, although we know not from exactly where.

Samuel and Ethel quickly had two boys, our father, Milton, and his brother, Alex. Samuel, although young, started a millinery business and soon had three shops selling haberdashery in the front and making hats in the room behind. Their speciality was extravagant constructions made from the feathers of birds of paradise. In 1918, when our father was only five, Samuel died in the Spanish flu epidemic and Ethel was left, a single mother of two, speaking only Yiddish, in charge of the business.

Desperate for security in this relatively new country where she found herself, Ethel soon married again, this time to a character called Murray Gottlieb. Since he could speak and write English and she assumed knew what he was doing, she hoped that he would be a help with her millinery business and her boys. But by all accounts he was a complete dolt and eventually the fledgling hat empire that Samuel Shulman had created collapsed, and Ethel spent her life with a man who was considerably less intelligent than she was.

An early picture of Ethel shows her with Samuel – he a serious, good-looking and unspeakably young fellow with small, unrimmed spectacles and a buttonhole; perhaps this was their wedding portrait. She looks quite like me. Round-faced, with heavy-lidded eyes and lustrous dark hair coiled above and behind her head, she is wearing a high-necked lace collar above a pin-tucked bodice. Neither looks at the camera, which is curious for a formal portrait of the time. They stand side by side – contemplative, as if immersed in their thoughts rather than in the act of being photographed. A couple arrived in an utterly new world, hoping to escape the prejudice, poverty and violence of the old. Another, taken several years later, shows her alone as the proud milliner wearing one of her flamboyant hats.

*Our grandmother Ethel in one of the birds-of-paradise
hats designed in her shop, 1925*

Ethel's Resident Aliens Border Crossing Identification Card from 1948 gives her address as 7916 Romain St, Los Angeles and has her signature in brown ink, Ethel Gottlieb. By then she would have been 57 and in the passport-sized picture her hair is white and she wears horn-rimmed spectacles. She and I share the jowls and downturn slope of the lips that age brings, but she appears a woman who takes care of herself. Although in the relatively few images that we have of her she looks quite stocky, this ID card reveals that she was the same height as me but 15lbs lighter!

How different her life was to mine. I have remained in the city of my birth for over 60 years and had the luxury of a good education, friends I have known since childhood, a happy family life and a successful career. I have been able to enjoy the kind of security and privilege that Ethel could not imagine. I have known no religious persecution, my family has not dispersed and I've never had to create myself in the image of a different society to that I once knew. I have not had to decide whether to cling on to my roots or look determinedly forward, in the way of so many immigrants who deliberately block out nostalgia to help them assimilate. Ethel had none of my certainties, and her decisions were often based on survival, taking one step in life after the other, not through choice but pragmatism.

She would, I am sure, have been proud and no doubt amazed by my being at the only formal occasion where I did wear a hat. Not perhaps exactly a hat, more of a headdress. But it served the same purpose of showing respect. It was concocted for me by Kate Halfpenny for the wedding of Prince William and Catherine Middleton, and in a mixture of dark blue chiffon and grosgrain with an antique diamanté decoration was designed to go with the blue Christopher Kane outfit I planned to wear. For the wedding of the future King of England, even I felt I should wear some kind of head covering.

I was invited because I had played a minuscule part in the proceedings. When the engagement was announced there was immediate interest in who would design the royal wedding dress. As Editor-in-Chief of *Vogue*, I was asked for my advice. Naturally I was hugely flattered and scrambled together a list of designers that I thought might be appropriate, bringing pictures of their work to Clarence House where I was to meet the duchess.

I remember her arriving in the large, gracious room and thinking her so much taller and slimmer than I had imagined. She had even then a poise that was quite startling for a young woman who was only at the beginning of her journey with The Firm. She was keen to listen to what I had to say, asking questions as we went through the candidates. It was clear that the chosen name should be British, but it was less clear whether it should be a fashion designer or somebody who specialized in bridal wear.

We sat on a sofa and discussed the various options, piles of pictures scattered on the floor. As we talked I began to realize that my favourite was Alexander McQueen, a label which at that point, shortly after McQueen's horribly untimely death, was newly in the hands of Sarah Burton. I thought that the level of extraordinary craftsmanship and their tradition of working with symbolism would be up to the task, that Sarah and she would get on as women, and that it would be terrific to have a relatively untraditional fashion house given this privilege.

I also thought Vivienne Westwood would make something gorgeous, although I was less sure about how she would feel about dealing with the intricate diplomacy involved with the royals. And I felt that Erdem Moralioglu, then still a relative newcomer to international fashion, would create a beautiful gown, though I was concerned whether his then-fledgling operation would be able to handle the vast security needed around the whole thing. And then I left. I didn't mention the meeting to anyone and I didn't hear anything more.

Months later, as I sat in the nave of Westminster Abbey awaiting the royal bride's arrival, I was obviously curious about what she had eventually chosen. I, like everyone else there, entertained myself during a long wait by watching who else had been invited. It was a total mix. Politicans in the row opposite, a heavily pregnant Victoria Beckham with her husband David, and nearby Cally Palmer, CEO of the Royal Marsden hospital. A few minutes before Catherine Middleton entered the Great West Door, a text pinged through from my colleague Sacha Forbes: 'It's McQueen!' She was unaware that it would have a particular resonance for me. I lay no claim to being anything other than one of many sources of that decision, but all the same I was thrilled at being a small speck in the picture of this particular moment in history.

My father wasn't alive by this point, and I was sad not to be able to regale him with what exactly happened on that day. He would have enjoyed the idea of one of his offspring at that occasion. He left Canada and Ethel during the Second World War, travelling to Britain as part of the Canadian military, and never returned. He rarely spoke of his childhood or his mother, and we have learned little of life in the Jewish enclave where he was brought up. But he always wore hats: fedoras, trilbies, a Borsalino. He would wear them to theatre first nights which he attended as the London *Evening Standard*'s theatre critic, where he took notes on a shorthand pad in ballpoint pen. He sometimes had a quick snooze in his seat, which like all critics' seats would be at the end of the row, allowing for a quick getaway to start on the overnight review. Every weekend he wore a flat white cap to play his regular tennis.

In the hall of the flat where we were brought up, his hats were kept on top of a bookshelf, ready to be put on as he walked out of the front door. I don't know that he ever threw one away. After he died, my brother took one of his treasured trilbies and had it cast in dark bronze. It still lives on that shelf.

7.

Indigo

As young children – that is, me, my sister, Nicky, and my brother, Jason – we were taken by our father, Milton, every Saturday morning on an expedition to buy comics and have a Coca-Cola. It was the envy of our friends and the treat of the week. Between the Sloane Square newsstand, where we would be bought whatever comics we wanted, and our home, there was a stretch of the route where it was possible to climb up onto a low wall that bordered the front garden of the houses and walk along it. The wall was about a metre high and the coping stone that topped it perhaps half that width. But it seemed, at the time, to be high enough to elicit (at least on my part, because I have always been a total wimp when it comes to anything physical) a thrill of danger, of precariousness.

As we ran along the wall or the pavement, occasionally holding our father's hand, we might sing, and one of our regular songs was 'I Can Sing a Rainbow', which wasn't a great song by any standards but provided an excuse to teach us the colours of the rainbow, which he did on that Saturday morning walk. 'ROYGBIV,' he would say, each time he mentioned the rainbow. 'That's how you remember the colours.' Although in his pronunciation, which was Canadian (and how many of us can describe a Canadian accent?), it sounded like ROYG A BIV. Red, Orange, Yellow, Green, Blue, INDIGO, Violet.

Indigo? What was indigo? Something perhaps to do with the Red Indians, as they were then called in TV Westerns? Those Cheyenne, Apache or Comanche, whose feathered headdresses and terrifying arrows were way more exciting than any aspect of the cowboys. At any rate indigo did not appear something straightforward like red, yellow or green. It was unusual and exotic.

My six-year-old self had the right idea. Indigo is not at all straightforward. Referred to by some as blue gold, indigo is a rare and precious dye.

A sign of the power of indigo is that it still exists. Because, if you look at where indigo is positioned between blue and violet on Isaac Newton's colour spectrum, it would be easy to simply skip it and call it blue. And in recent iterations of the rainbow, like that of the early Apple logo and now Gay Pride, exactly that has happened. It has been removed, leaving the arc with only six colours.

But indigo is more than a colour. You need only to experience the gloaming, that brief period on a clear night before the light disappears, when there is a trace of this deep, electric blue. Or spot it at dawn, as the sun rises while the moon is still up, to realize that indigo is also a feeling. It's complex and almost impossible to categorize. The best aural rendering of it is Charles Mingus's version of Duke Ellington's 'Mood Indigo'. The instruments march to their own beat – the insistent shuffle of the drum, the physicality of the deep bass and the swirling chords of piano. It's fascinating and engaged with life and far too rich to be melancholy despite Ellington's lyrics (not included in this purely instrumental rendition), 'You ain't been blue until you've had that mood indigo'.

Of course none of this was or is relevant to my own love of indigo. The first indigo clothes I was aware of hung in our mother's wardrobe – a built-in, white, double-doored depository from which she would pull outfits each morning to dress for work. Her job in the mid-Seventies was Editor of *Brides* magazine, and she particularly liked an Issey Miyake outfit of indigo-dyed skirt, shirt and trousers. This was several years before the Japanese triumvirate of Miyake, Rei Kawakubo and Yohji Yamamoto became the heroes of the fashion avant-garde.

Her skirt was full and gathered at the waist, falling to mid-calf. The shirt was Mao-collared and straight, without a waist or bust, and the trousers were wide and loose. My father hated them all. Said she looked like a dustman in them. I certainly found them drab and somehow irritating.

As if she felt that she didn't have to look pretty. That walking around in these baggy trousers and mandarin-collared shirt, she didn't have to bother. Bother with what? Bother with the kind of cosy femininity of maternal dressing? Bother with getting her hair done, because along with the indigo outfits she had started to wear a bandana over her hair? Bother with whether our dad liked how she looked? Would there be no end to what she might not bother with? Might that, ultimately, be us?

And then a couple of years later the utility chic of my mother's outfit had no place in the world she occupied, one of journalism and the arts. When the Eighties took root in all their unfettered encouragement of financial ambition, professional careers, property ownership and the tearing down, literally, of the walls between East and West, nobody I knew wore that kind of ethnic-tinged clothing. No. We were much more likely to be wearing suits and batwing sleeves and leggings. Cone heels and permed hair.

Although much Eighties style was deliberately hard-edged and corporate, in its ambition to equalize the playing field between the sexes it shared the same desire of liberation from gender stereotype as my mother's indigo outfit. But a young woman of that time, wanting to get on and take advantage of the work options that were opening up all over the place – or appeared to be – was not going to

Our mother in Herefordshire wearing her bandana, 1973

drape herself in an indigo sack or baggy trousers. The last thing we wanted to look like was a field worker in some far-flung communist regime. There was, after all, the newly termed glass ceiling to crack.

'Seems So Long Ago, Nancy' was the title of a Leonard Cohen song and a headline I put on an interview with Nancy Reagan in *Vogue* in 1989, accompanying a Bruce Weber portrait of Nancy in a pale suit that epitomized everything that indigo was not. And all of that does seem so long ago. But 30 years on, my own wardrobe is filled with every scrap of indigo I can afford – indigo dyes are still expensive. I have a loose patchwork indigo dress I love. At first glance it appears shapeless but when on the body it actually gives me a narrow shoulder and back. It's a little arty. It's hugely comfortable. It could never be thought exactly fashionable but fits perfectly with my current identity as somebody who was part of one world, a world where fashion was central. And who has moved to another world, where it is satellite.

The other day I visited my mother and asked her about those original clothes of hers. She still had them hung in the same wardrobe. We pulled them out and laid them on her bed. The shirt had lost some of the blue of the dye and faded to a slightly greyer shade than I remembered. But other than that, they were just as they had been when she had bought them. Timeless.

8.

The Chanel Jacket

I was gifted two Chanel jackets by the label's London press office soon after my arrival at *Vogue*. Bernadette was the woman who ran the team there at that time, and she was the epitome of Chanel chic. She was slim and tall with a lightly tanned complexion and short blonde hair that never looked flat or messy but always crisply attractive. She was of course always dressed in Chanel, which she managed to wear rather than have it wear her. It would have been hard to envisage her in anything else.

One of these jackets was a long-line lilac double-breasted number with wide lapels and gold buttons, the other a single-breasted black, and they would have cost about £1,000 at that time, 1992, in one of the boutiques. The label was the epitome of status dress for the successful magazine executive.

As a journalist, wearing Chanel, more likely than not, indicated you were well enough regarded by the house to have been given the clothes, since most of us in the UK could never have afforded such things on salary alone. I remember hearing that there were editors who would arrive in their hotel rooms in Paris for the shows to find the wardrobes stuffed with Chanel hanging bags, though it was not something I ever experienced.

When I was appointed to edit *Vogue*, Jonathan Newhouse, then chairman of the company, asked how much I spent on clothes in a year. I had no idea. It was a calculation I had never even thought of doing but I was pretty sure that, whatever the sum was, it would not sound very impressive to him. This was not a company where thrift in matters of personal appearance was rewarded. So I told him that I thought it was about £4,000, which was probably around triple what I truly spent.

Only later did I learn from my immediate boss Nicholas Coleridge that it was at this point that Jonathan wondered, no doubt not for the last time, whether he had hired the right person to edit the leading fashion magazine in the country. Somebody who, as he saw it, spent such a paltry amount. Certainly, it indicated that he couldn't really know how much his editors were earning, or must have assumed that they had other means of financing their wardrobes.

And I, also not for the last time, realized that there was a deep and potentially troubling gap between the economic realities of those who worked on fashion magazines and the veneer of expensive style that we appeared to possess. Would I always feel under pressure to look wealthier than

I was? Was my real life not going to measure up to the person I would be assumed to be?

As part of my initial *Vogue* salary I was given a clothes allowance of £4,000 – that it was the same amount as I had told them I spent was a coincidence. It seemed a fortune. It was. But it wasn't going to keep me in the Chanel wardrobe that other high-powered *Vogue* editors of the time were wearing daily. Angelica Blechschmidt, Editor of German *Vogue*, a Cruella-de-Vil lookalike, supplemented her always black Chanel with floor-length fur. The ebullient freelance fashion editor Carlyne Cerf de Dudzeele, a friend of Karl Lagerfeld, hung Chanel bags from her body like they were Christmas baubles. Even my own fashion director when I arrived at the magazine, Sarajane Hoare, was rarely spotted out of a Chanel principal-boy look.

A few weeks into my job I had lunch with Anna Wintour, one of Chanel's biggest fans. The fact that my predecessor at *Vogue*, Liz Tilberis, had moved to New York with the promise of a vast budget to relaunch the rival *Harper's Bazaar* magazine and had put on contract two of *Vogue*'s leading photographers, Patrick Demarchelier and Peter Lindbergh, had meant that war was declared. All the photographers were going to have to decide whose side they were on and those choosing to work with *Harper's Bazaar* would not be allowed to work with us. Anna considered it worthwhile meeting me to encourage me in this plan; a plan which made my first year at the magazine extremely difficult by us losing several of our most valued photographers.

She arrived at Le Caprice restaurant like a firework in a brilliant orange mini-skirted Chanel suit, thick shiny black tights and, of course, her thick, shiny, black sunglasses. I remember her briskly telling me that I must make sure that I was given all the money I needed to do what I had to do with the magazine. Advice that I am not sure I ever succeeded in achieving. It didn't tally with the fact that as soon as I arrived I had been told that I must lose staff and cut costs.

Anna looked marvellous in her Chanel, which confirmed for me that this particular style was owned by a previous cadre of magazine editors. I was not going to enter that competition. An arsenal of Chanel jackets which marked one as wealthy and successful was never going to feel quite like 'me', I thought. But, as in so many things, I was wrong.

Chanel, although demanding a certain rigour, is based on the founder's philosophy that women should dress to do what they wished. That they should feel enabled rather than hampered by their clothes. Coco Chanel's initial soft tweed fitted like a cardigan and the pockets allowed women to carry what they needed, their hands freed from a bag. The hems were anchored by a gilt chain so that they hung immaculately and, like all Chanel's designs, the way they looked from behind was given equal regard as how they appeared from the front.

By the time I arrived at *Vogue* Karl Lagerfeld had taken over as the creative director of the house, ten years after the founder's death. At the tail end of the Eighties he had taken the staples of her designs, the navy and white, the gilt, the tweeds, the costume jewellery, the quilting, and with a more-is-more attitude had made the label fizz. Young women craved the clothes that only two decades ago had been deemed outmoded and elderly by the standards of the Sixties and Seventies. Now here they were again but this time lively and newly desirable. A Chanel jacket layered with layers of pearls and faux jewels would be seen on Linda Evangelista, Cindy Crawford, Naomi Campbell – the epoch's supermodels – in real life as well as at the fashion shoots.

Unlike many fashion houses, Chanel's ready-to-wear collections still make money, and the jacket is still a mainstay, season after season. Sometimes it is lengthened, while other times it is more like a bolero. Sometimes it is encrusted in jewellery and sometimes it is lightweight, like a simple cardigan.

Lunch at the Wolseley with Taylor Swift and a Chanel jacket, 2015

Those jackets I was originally gifted are no longer in my wardrobe. I don't know what I did with them. But I still own a few. They are all short – one with delicious frayed cream satin at the lapels and cuffs, one in a dark grey and white check, another a navy boucle with sloping shoulders, decorated with gunmetal buttons. I regard them as an insurance policy. I feel safer in the knowledge that they are there for me to wear should I need to impress a prospective employer of some kind. I know that although they are decades old they are still an effective shorthand. I can put on a Chanel jacket and a pair of heels and immediately I can be seen, in the wider world, as somebody who, at some point, edited *Vogue*.

9.

The Hairdresser's Gown

Consider this: a room where people sit in rows of chairs in front of mirrors, swathed in drab material that disguises their clothes and their shape, leaving only their heads exposed, waiting like storeroom dummies to be worked upon. Welcome to the hairdresser.

There's a massive contradiction in the fact that we visit our hairdresser to hopefully improve our appearance yet throughout the process wear something that is without a single iota of charm or grace, and does absolutely no favours to any single part of our anatomy. I've often wondered whether hairdresser's gowns are deliberately designed to make us look so grim at the start of the process in order that we will consider anything that follows an improvement.

My earliest experience of the hairdresser was being taken by my mother to hers. For many years she would have a weekly shampoo and set, her hair under the drying hood in large rollers, at Alan Spiers, a hairdresser at the north end of Berkeley Square, in the West End of London. It was a gracious townhouse and the salon was on the ground floor with a large window that looked out over the square garden towards The Ritz on Piccadilly. Sometimes Mum would take us children along with her because, I imagine, she had nowhere else to leave us. We might be perched on a chair beside her, but most often we would spend the hour or so of her appointment hiding in the darkly mysterious cupboard near the reception desk that housed the gowns and, more interestingly, the manicurist's trolley, with its selection of gorgeous peaked bottles filled with pinks, scarlets and crimson varnishes with names like Fire and Ice.

Even as a child I realized that hairdressers were places of transformation. They manipulate the combination of carbon, nitrogen, oxygen, sulphur and hydrogen, bonded with amino acids, that travel along follicles below our skin to emerge as hair, the dead matter on our scalps. Dead, yes, but even so, hairdressers know they are working with the most instantly potent element of our appearance. Hair packs a massive punch. We read into it power, virility, youth, health. And it is all those things and so much more that we are hoping to address when we visit the hairdresser. Donning the gown is the entry process. Each snip, tong, tint, comb and curl changes so much more than how that dead matter looks. We think, or at least we do quite often, that it will change our lives.

When I was 11, my mother, for reasons best known to herself, decided I should be given the haircut of the moment. This was a short geometric crop, invented by Vidal Sassoon and worn by people like Twiggy and Mary Quant and a television actress I liked called Adrienne Posta. It was not, however, a good look for a round faced 11-year-old who had to wear a straw boater as part of her school uniform.

Snip, snip, onto the floor of Alan Spiers tumbled my shoulder-length brown hair. And the memory of how it felt to watch my hair pooling around the chair and then to emerge with this dramatic cut was damaging enough to keep me out of hairdressers for the greater part of 25 years, until I joined *Vogue*. I felt far more at ease with hair that appeared to have nothing done to it than I ever did – or still in general do – with hair that is 'done'.

My hair simply grew and grew. I fiddled with and tore off the split ends (something I remember once being obsessed by but which I have not given a second's thought to for many decades). And because it was straight I could just cut bits off it from time to time in the bathroom. I learned that conditioner was not, as I had suspected until I was about 13 when reading magazine questionnaires that posited 'How often do you use conditioner? a) weekly, b) monthly, c) never', something mysterious to do with sex, and started to pour it by the bottleload onto my hair. I slept in wet plaits to give it waves, caked it in disgusting smelling henna, and bought things called Molton Browners which were basically padded pipe cleaners that you could twist your hair around. I broke my no salon rule when I left university to get a perm, which I hoped would make me look like Maria Schneider in Antonioni's *The Passenger*, but after that grew out it was back to the long and straight.

For most women and many men the salon is a place of respite – even for some akin to a church. It is an escape from the demands of others, a refuge that offers in its own way a type of deliverance and, ultimately, a better you. The moment of putting on the gown is where you hand yourself over with a passive trust and more than a dash of hope.

You go in one person and emerge, quite possibly, and certainly that is the plan, as someone new.

Why else would I or anyone be prepared to spend hours in that hideous gown within which even the most swan-like neck is disguised? It's why we sit there, fiddling on iPads, reading magazines, chatting loudly on the phone (if you are particularly annoying) and occasionally glancing along the row of endlessly reflecting mirrors at a lot of unrecognizable people with heads of silver foil wrappers, towel turbans and waxy dark paste tints or tilted back against a porcelain sink as an invariably black T shirted assistant showers and scrubs, showers and scrubs, massages and squeezes. And where every now and again we spot someone, somewhere further along the row of mirrors, looking just a little bit like us, with the same shade of hair of the same length but with a vague jawline and a disconsolate droop about the mouth, and discover, as we move our hand or adjust our chair, that, Oh God, it's me. Do I really look like that? Followed swiftly by, Thank God I'm here and something can be done about it.

A good hairdresser is not just somebody who faffs around with your hair. They are the depositary of confessions and aspirations. Great hairdressers, and I count mine in this, are masters of the conversational recipe that mixes the perfect amount of gossip, speculation, reassurance and authority. And we so want to believe in that higher authority.

Personally, the words I least want to hear coming out of my hairdresser's mouth are, What do you think? Should there be a bit more fullness? Is it time for a whole new look? Should it have a bit more choppiness, or should we do something radical like try a fringe? Do you think it would be good to go a bit lighter? I want to be told. I want them to do the thinking for me, and then to come up with the correct answer. I want to trust that they will know what they should do to make sure that at the end of the process, when that gown is thankfully removed, and I can see myself in my own clothes and no longer looking like a member of a sinister cult, I will step onto the street feeling that the world is a better place because now I have great hair.

10

Brooches, Badges and Pins

Pinned insignia are all about membership of a group, and my earliest experience of wearing them was not a happy one, at the weekly Brownies meeting held in the crypt of the local church. Even now, occasionally hearing the sound of the bells there chiming 5pm reminds me of the anticipated misery.

In those days Brownie packs were divided into groups. I was an Elf, and an extremely disconsolate one at that. Our motto could not have been less personally appropriate: 'I am a happy little elf, helping others before myself.'

Our blue Elf badge had to be sewn onto our brown cotton uniform. It was supposed to be the first of many. As the weeks passed it seemed that everyone else's dress was becoming covered in badges proclaiming their ability to make rice pudding, tie complex knots and build a fire. But not mine. Thinking back, it can't be possible that I was really unable to do any of the decreed tasks – although even now knots and stitching are not my forte – but I hated the enforced need to achieve. I resented the idea that you had to perform in a certain way to have achievement acknowledged. So my uniform remained a desert, empty of the insignia that were a key part of the Brownie experience, and showing to anyone sitting there beside me, cross-legged on the linoleum floor, that I was a hopeless Brownie.

Badges are the utilitarian siblings of the decorative brooch, both known as pins in the United States. They often demonstrate allegiance and signify triumph of one kind or another. You pin your colours to the mast. You wear a badge of honour. To wear your heart on your sleeve is surely to wear it like a badge for all to see. But in their overt signalling of membership they can also be malign emblems of prejudice and fear, such as the yellow star forced on Jews by the Nazis or the sinister hooded pin given to Klu Klux Klan members at Jim Crow rallies celebrating racial segregation.

Brooches may not convey quite the same obvious messages but they share with the badge the fact that nobody ever wears one accidentally. Displaying them is the most deliberate of actions. You have to make an active choice in the positioning, participate in their attachment and of course their removal. The clasps are frequently fiddly, and often the wearer has to stab at fabric and weave the pin with difficulty through stiff cloth. You don't just kind of slip a brooch on without noticing.

Brooches are the sophisticated elder sisters of the family. They were originally fastenings, made from thorns and flint, but as they evolved and became cast in metals and gems they also came to demonstrate wealth and status. Silent and still, unlike necklaces and bracelets, they don't have the kind of distracting jingle jangle of pendulous jewellery. Yet they are equally capable of making a statement and can carry a louder voice than any other piece of personal ornamentation.

The other day, in the guise of research for this book, I spent a morning rewatching one of my favourite films, *Bad Timing* by the director Nicolas Roeg. This tale of sexual obsession was released in the Eighties with Theresa Russell, Roeg's then wife, playing the wayward Milena, and Art Garfunkel the psychoanalyst Alex, whom she enthrals. The costumes for the film were designed by Marit Allen who had previously been a successful *Vogue* fashion editor, and in the choice of Milena's clothes Marit cleverly enhances the viewer's understanding of this unpredictable, charismatic, chaotic girl who's both femme fatale and needy, drunk victim.

These costumes are always block colour – carmine, orange, yellow, cobalt, cerise. And she wears brooches. Ostentatious, loud, unmissable brooches – a lavender bird, a Bakelite rockabilly, a diamante circle that clasps her mink jacket – all of which are lingered on by the camera in adoring close-up.

Theresa Russell and Nicolas Roeg on the set of Bad Timing, *1980*

Her outfits are part of the colourful, shiny world across the Iron Curtain. Our first sight of her is when she appears to be leaving her older Czech husband at the checkpoint between Czechoslovakia and Austria. Milena wears a black coat with a bronze woman's hand pinned above her left breast. The long elegant fingers are tipped in scarlet, at the base is a thick chain bracelet and on the fourth finger a deep green, faux emerald ring. The pin is coming away from her coat, and just before her husband walks away, apparently handing her over to her freedom, he deliberately pushes the pin back into the fabric so that the brooch is fixed in its place. If we knew then what we later learn, we would see that the brooch is as firm as their relationship. The brooch tells the whole story.

The early Eighties was a time when costume jewellery, which had slipped out of style, began again to be in fashion. My then boyfriend gave me a weighty silver brooch in the shape of an Indian elephant decorated with coloured glass – a green eye, candy floss pink bridle, clear glass toes. I wore it most of the time. For several years. Until, as with so many accessories, it suddenly looked old-fashioned. As if I had no idea that time had moved on and that we did not now wear Indian elephants or fake deco and nouveau or, really, any faintly nostalgic brooches at all.

At a party last year I noticed a Lanvin star pinned onto my goddaughter's black mini dress. She had been given it as a 30th birthday present by her mother Flora, a successful historian. It was Flora who had first drawn my attention to the role of brooches, telling me that when she does book tours she always wears a 'pin'. It gives people something to look at – something to ask her about. Which they often do. How beautiful your pin is! Where did you get your pin? It's an easy conversational point and a way of talking about appearance which is somehow less personal or pointed than it is when talking about a necklace or earrings. Perhaps because pins/brooches are worn on cloth and not on flesh.

The grandmistress of the pin is the American diplomat Madeleine Albright whose collection of pins is so large and fascinating that it warranted an exhibition at New York's Metropolitan Museum of Art. As America's ambassador to the UN and later Secretary of State, she employed her collection to great effect. In the show's catalogue *Read my Pins: Stories from a Diplomat's Jewel Box* she writes of her lifelong relationship with brooches, from the student days when a girl would wear her boyfriend's fraternity house pin to show off their connection through to the diamond eagle she bought herself as a gift when she was named Secretary of State.

Most of us use a brooch as a decoration to liven up a plain outfit, but Albright used hers as a diplomatic tool. She put on the Three Wise Monkeys (see no evil, hear no evil, speak no evil) to meet Putin to discuss his denial of human rights violations in Chechnya, and she wore a gold and diamond serpent to meet Iraqi officials after being branded 'an unparalleled serpent' by the press of the Saddam Hussein regime. Her pins could say what she might not have wanted to verbally articulate. They were the ultimate in soft power. Similar, some might say, to the large spider brooch Lady Hale wore to deliver the 2019 British Supreme Court verdict on whether Boris Johnson's suspension of parliament was lawful.

I often wonder how much my loathing of my early Brownie experience determined my reaction to formalized success and achievement. Those badges which I failed to earn were intended to be shown off. You did not just receive your cloth badge and shove it into a drawer in your bedroom. The point was to publicly display your skill.

However, I have done exactly that, and hidden away two magnificent pins since the day they were awarded. The first, the Order of the British Empire, which I received for services to the magazine industry, hangs on a grosgrain ribbon in a shade of dark salmon. It was pinned onto my jacket by the Queen at Buckingham Palace in June 2007.

The other, the more senior Commander of the British Empire, for services to fashion journalism, has a slightly longer and wider ribbon and the arms of the same shaped cross are this time in blue enamel. That was pinned onto my coat by the Duke of Cambridge the year after I left *Vogue*. For some reason, you are told that if you wish to wear them in public you should apply for a miniature version rather than wear these large medals. And I haven't. So I only see them very occasionally. Hardly ever. Since how often does one go around looking into leather boxes stuffed in a scarf drawer?

This is no doubt part of a very English reticence about showing off, the same reticence that relegates framed certificates to the walls of the downstairs loo rather than silver frames on the mantelpiece. Certainly, not wishing to appear boastful is not a condition shared by the European wearers of France's Légion d'honneur or the Italian Cavaliere, similar honours which are worn as discreet lapel pins on their honourees' everyday wear.

But everyone has a very personal take on how much they want to flaunt achievements. Perhaps, as I grow older, I will decide the time has come to wear those orders out and about like the medals of the marching veterans on Armistice Day. Perhaps I will ditch the protocol and indulge in the glorious fact that I own them, and instead of adopting my current fey coyness I will display them proudly on my left breast to go shopping. The best and the brightest pins I could ever hope to wear.

II.

The Little Black Dress

A black dress. The Little Black Dress. The LBD. Somewhere along the way a piece of clothing became one of the most famous acronyms of the Western world – three letters containing an imagined universe of sophistication, chic, allure.

It's unclear where the deliberate acronym was launched, but an early citing is in the *Sydney Morning Herald* of May 1977 when the In My Fashion column comments: 'it would be pointless to try to estimate the number of times one has been saved from fashion disaster by looking in the wardrobe and reaching for that same l.b.d.' There you have it – the notion of a simple, useful and yet fashionable black dress. Surely an essential part of the kit if you were Editor-in-Chief of the most famous fashion magazine in the world. But I didn't own one.

Within nine months of my arriving at *Vogue* the prevailing fashion of the time had been exploded by the now infamous Marc Jacobs for Perry Ellis collection. During one 15-minute show in New York Fashion Week, Jacobs had blown the previous epoch of sassy power dressing clean out of the water. His parade of models wearing striped scarves, beanie hats, plaid shirts, long slip dresses and Converse trainers was a rare moment where the fashion dial was conclusively reset. The slick, vampy, leggy looks of the later Eighties were replaced by the supermodels looking like the very young women they actually still were. Seemingly bare of make-up, they slouched along the floor, rather than on the traditional raised catwalk, before the fashion press and buyers. And in the who-cares, downbeat stance of grunge they bore an uncanny resemblance to the London schoolgirls I and my friends had been 20 years before.

Unfortunately, much as it was a style that resonated entirely with my personal heartland, as *Vogue* Editor I was not expected to turn up at work looking that way. The grunge movement may have marked a shift in fashion, but it was also an example of the parallel universes at play in that world. In the pages of fashion magazines, in the work of fashion photographers, in the casting of different young models, it was a new reality, but in the everyday, executive halls of fashion where I spent most of my time it was no way to dress if you were to be taken seriously. No, I was expected to look more put-together, polished, expensive. And, to be realistic, at 35 I was probably a bit old to suddenly pitch up in grunge regalia.

As it happened, although the grunge revolution reduced the previous high fashion staples of shoulder pads and short skirts, gilt buttons and principal boy leggings to a pile of rubble, it was not only in professional life that grunge didn't go mainstream. It was never a commercial success. Very soon, within a year, the rubble was swept away and a new, more obviously glamorous and aspirational style reasserted itself. And, as it also happened, the LBD was one of the pillars of this resurrection.

The London designer Catherine Walker, a woman who did not have a single grunge cell in her body, was at that point the go-to designer for formal dressing. She had been a favourite of my predecessor, Liz Tilberis – a fashion editor who, from the moment she gained the Editor's chair, ditched the white shirt and chinos she previously wore and adopted Chanel and Catherine Walker as her uniform. Walker was also a favourite of my deputy editor, the late Anna Harvey. Having been given the role of unofficial style advisor to the young Princess of Wales, Anna had steered her in Walker's direction and soon she became Diana's couturier of choice. After a few months of my being the new incumbent of the *Vogue* role, Catherine offered to make me something to wear.

I remember being torn by this generous offer, because although I appreciated the gesture – Catherine Walker's clothes were sophisticated and expensive and luxurious – I had never seen anything designed by her that I could imagine myself wearing. Walker's clothes were for women that I was not. They were for rangy upper-class Brits who could carry off wools and tweeds without looking like Tweedledum – or Dee. They suited neat bobbed hair or chignons rather than the long often-tangled tresses of my own head. Her long evening gowns were at their most glorious in pale colours like mint, beige, cream, which don't suit my colouring, heavily beaded, almost regal in their need to be carried off rather than simply worn.

So it was with not a little trepidation that I arrived in her small showroom just off London's Fulham Road to be fitted for a gift that was so imposing I was terrified that I was going to let it down. In all honesty I suspect that Catherine, a contained, elegant, pale-faced French woman, was equally apprehensive about how she was going to make this work.

She showed me around the relatively small centre of operations. In the room that fronted the street there were samples rails of light boucle tweed suits and dresses for the races or dinners at The Ritz. There were cocktail dresses to be worn with multi-strand pearl chokers and fine black tights for gatherings in the stucco terraces of Kensington and Belgravia or Paris's Avenue Foch and

Manhattan's Upper East Side. Then deeper into the back was a room filled with sumptuous evening gowns, hung in their cellophane protection, for the rarefied world of galas and black tie events. At that time, there were far fewer such occasions – red carpet dressing was still to become the mass entertainment that it now is – and the need for these wonderful gowns was, even for the Editor of *Vogue*, occasional to say the very least.

Catherine was much kinder than I had expected and very reassuring. Between us we speedily realized that none of these prototypes were going to be for me. After all, if Catherine was to make me an outfit, she wanted it to be something that I would be able to wear often. Not something that would lurk in a suit carrier at the furthest end of a wardrobe, waiting forlornly for a moment that never arrived.

And so it was that I became the owner of a really beautiful LBD. She suggested that she design one with a short matching coat, so that I could wear it to the office if need be and then on to drinks. It would be sleeveless and so suitable for warm weather and well-heated restaurants and parties, while the coat would give it a life in colder weather. It was to be a fail-safe garment that would make me feel ready to face whoever and whatever I had to face, in the knowledge that it fitted perfectly because it was a one-off made only for my body. The armholes cut to be the most flattering, the neckline adjusted in a perfect span of my collarbone, the tapering at the waist designed to make me appear more streamlined, giving me the most attractive shape it could. Not too short a torso, not too broad a hip.

It was its apparent simplicity which enabled the LBD to rise as an unlikely phoenix from the ashes of grunge. Stripped back and understated, it was a fashion piece that provided a bridge spanning the remnants of Eighties go-getting polish and the anti-conspicuous aspiration of grunge, to land us in the chic minimalism of the mid-Nineties. But in this sparse incarnation it differed hugely from possibly the most famous LBD of them all; the LBD now lodged in our collective consciousness and endlessly cited as the apotheosis of LBDs – the Givenchy creation worn by Audrey Hepburn in the opening scene of *Breakfast at Tiffany's*.

The Little Black Dress had gained recognition as a one-stop route to chic for all occasions – but Hepburn's was not such a dress at all. That full-length satin sheath with a side split and an ornate neckline, even without the heavenly collar of pearls that accessorized it, could never be worn outside a nightclub or a party.

There is debate about who launched the classic little black dress. Some say it was the British designer Molyneux

Dovima wearing an LBD in American Vogue, *1952*

– in 1928 *The Times* reports of his collection, 'For the afternoon there are simple little black dresses with frilled and draped skirts' – others attribute it to a Coco Chanel dress featured in a 1926 American *Vogue*. Either or neither may be true, but what is certain is that, at this time, black began to be worn less formally during the day and black dresses became fashionable rather than being considered the clothing of housemaids or the drapes of mourning.

The zeitgeist of the mid-Twenties was questioning and creative. After the end of the First World War, daily existence in Britain and Europe was determined by attempts to patch together a world from the debris. Although the war was over, the basic necessities of life were hard to come by and the world was very different to how it had been before. When a society is primarily immersed in the act of surviving there is little time to ponder questions about who we are or what we want to be. That is a luxury of peace.

By the Twenties, though, the social order was recovering and there was a growing desire among artists and intellectuals to question society and its mores. Writers like Virginia Woolf and Radclyffe Hall were exploring gender, the new Surrealist movement offered a startlingly different vision, and speed – via the new air travel and the increasing ownership of the car – was transforming the way the world was viewed. Technologies in machinery and fabrics were adopted by a middle class who could no longer afford or need a domestic staff, and women in particular were living in a new world – one which had lost a generation of young men leaving many of them single and certainly needing to work. It was into this environment that the black dress – little or not – came of age. It became something that could be worn by everyone, everywhere, every day.

Over the years my collection of LBDs has expanded and more often than not they appear at social extremes – funerals and parties – but they are not worn everywhere, every day. An elderly man once told me of a conversation between himself and a Frenchman. The latter announced that Englishmen should always dress their wives in pale blue but look back, over their shoulder, at women in black.

Oberto Gili portrait, 1992

12.

White Shirts

On my 10th anniversary of editing *Vogue* my team put together a scrapbook as a gift. Inside the embossed blue leather cover was a collection of notes (reminiscences, compliments, jokes) and pictures from them and many of the designers I had worked with during that time: Alexander McQueen, Donna Karan, Michael Kors, Donatella Versace, Phoebe Philo, Calvin Klein, etc.

Somebody had found a box of old transparencies taken during my first summer at the magazine, by the Italian photographer Oberto Gili, and included one of the pictures. It was part of a set of publicity shots intended to show me as the kind of person who looked like the kind of person who was in charge. It was a headshot taken at a slight angle. I had a mane of thick dark hair, half pulled back and pinned up, the rest hanging loose, and I was wearing a white shirt. In the album it is captioned 'The White Shirt. We've never seen her in one before or since...'

Which was correct. But before then, before *Vogue*, I had certainly had my white shirt moment.

The Robert Mapplethorpe cover image of Patti Smith's first album, *Horses*, was seminal to my teens. There she

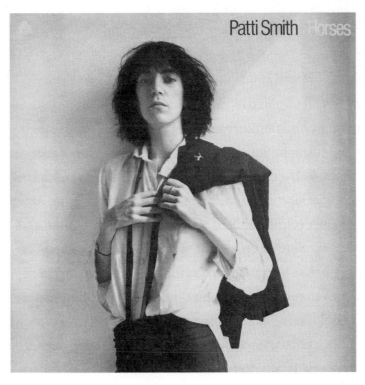

The inspiring portrait of Patti Smith by Robert Mapplethorpe, 1975

stood, the ultimate in androgyne insouciance, blowing away, in one shot, the flowing long-haired hippie ideal of femininity. She wears a white shirt, unbuttoned only at the neck, the cuffs rolled up, tucked into black trousers. A black jacket hangs over her shoulder and her trousers are so loose on her frame that they are held up with a pair of black braces. She stares at us defiantly, challenging us to accept this pre-punk urban style.

That autumn I was 18 and I saw her perform *Horses* at Hammersmith Odeon. After the show I took the underground home and decided that the only thing I ever really wanted to wear from that point forward was a loose white shirt. No matter that Patti Smith's white shirt hung from the skinniest torso, which was not the case of my own. No matter that her scratchy black bob, white skin and Modigliani neck lent her a patrician hauteur far from my round face and long hair. She was the person I wanted to look like. In fact, the person I wanted to be. A New York street urchin of indeterminate sexuality rather than a London private school girl trapped in an A-level curriculum.

As I recall, a white shirt wasn't a piece of clothing that I possessed, so it was off to the nearest church hall jumble sale to find a second-hand man's shirt as soon as possible. It's possible that such was my desperation to create this image, immediately, that I borrowed one from my father's wardrobe as an interim measure. But in truth I don't remember if that was the case or not. Of course Patti Smith's white shirt looked absolutely nothing like the white shirt I found in the piles of old clothes in the church hall, which would probably have been bundled into a charity bag by the wife of a man who wore a white shirt to work with his grey suit every day of the week and which had nothing remotely cool or sexy or gender bending about it. But it was my first white shirt.

How strange it now seems that, for the rest of my life, white shirts have come to represent almost everything that is the opposite of the ideals of that Mapplethorpe album cover. They signify order and neatness, professionalism and authority. When I chose to wear a white shirt for that Oberto Gili portrait, I was joining a monstrous regiment of executive female publicity shots. We know them so well, these images that stare out of the pages of magazines and newspapers, websites and press releases, hair a neat bob or at least a smooth blow-dry, a 'trust-me', even gaze or occasionally a warm smile, and often a manicured hand cupping the cheek – always a helpful tool in pushing away any unhelpful softness around the jaw. The white shirt is a symbol of unshowy competence and unlikely to draw any troll's vitriol on the basis of being too glamorous, or tacky. Share prices or mortgages look to be in safe hands with a woman in a white shirt, someone who, with the need to be judged as an appropriate person to be in charge, tends to veer towards the austere rather than exuberant when it comes to working clothes.

Professional dress even now, even after Michelle Obama's colourful, bare-armed contribution to First Lady dressing or Amal Clooney's sleek and undeniably glamorous appearance as she negotiates human rights with world leaders, is usually a tricky proposition. Appearing confident, feeling comfortable and maintaining any kind of joyfulness is testing. Let alone doing it day after day. Professional dressing is a Rubik's cube. All the pieces have to click into place at the same time: the right degree of attractiveness as opposed to overt sexuality, the right amount of attention to appearance as opposed to time-wasting vanity, an understanding of the status symbols of your particular environment without being a slave to them. No wonder that white shirts ride to the rescue, providing a blank canvas that can be tailored any number of ways. A sure-fire option for the table-up dressing (a phrase that I have loved ever since I first heard it, meaning only your top half is on view) of boardroom meetings, Skype and FaceTime, the white shirt is never going to let you down (unless you're unlucky enough not to have noticed that your pre-meeting coffee has drizzled down your front).

There are women who dedicate hours and hours to the search for the next white shirt. Satisfaction is always the next shop away. For the white shirt aficionado there is no such thing as enough, because luckily their objects of desire have an inbuilt obsolescence. The crispness, purity and brightness that make them so addictive never lasts, can only survive a certain number of washes or dry-cleans.

These pieces of clothing are masters of illusion, appearing to be so simple and artless while being one of the most high-maintenance items in a wardrobe – all that ironing, all that...whiteness.

Yes, that unadorned whiteness that is so often used by celebrities when they want to make a public statement. Meghan Markle wore her oversized white shirt and torn jeans for her first public appearance with Prince Harry, and Victoria Beckham wore one on the *Vogue* cover where she appeared surrounded by her flock of children under a tree – a mother superior rather than an ambitious designer. Alexa Chung wore hers standing on the catwalk at the end of her first fashion show, joining the uniform of female designers who use it on such occasions to say I-am-the-behind-the-scenes-worker-bee rather than a front row celebrity. White shirts are shorthand for: the real me. They escape the date stamp of fashion.

It's the same but different from the way that fashion stylists, who create memorable fashion pictures or style celebrity portraits, often themselves wear white shirts. Like make-up artists who rarely wear any make-up themselves, fashion editors often adopt a neutral uniform when they are at work. Jeans or a pair of black trousers and a white shirt are common on set. The sparse uniform acts as a blank space so that the subject of the picture – the model, the personality, the clothes – is unaffected by what the stylist is wearing. They can shine like jewels against black velvet without any distraction from the fashion stylist, the person who is there to assemble the image and not be part of it.

When we were children, my sister, who hated apples – a fruit we were always being urged to eat instead of another Mars Bar or to limit the time we would spend blowing pink Bazooka bubbles – would wail, staring glumly at a bowl of Golden Delicious, 'Lucky beggars liking apples.' And when I read, as I often do, of very stylish and successful women who have a huge collection of white shirts that they nominate as their go-to wardrobe item, I always think, 'Lucky beggars liking white shirts.' How lovely it would be to see them hanging there – a clean, crisp army at the ready.

I did once have a Karl Lagerfeld shirt ready and waiting, which I wore for a dinner at his house in Paris during a couture week in the Nineties. His home was one of those secret palaces in the city, hidden behind megalithic doors on the narrow pavements of the Left Bank which, when opened, reveal magnificent cobbled courtyards. Ballroom-sized rooms that would put the Buckingham Palace staterooms to shame slowly filled up with models, the odd couture buyer, some magazine editors and various celebrities who were in town.

Amazingly, I found myself seated next to Richard Gere, who ever since his appearance in *An Officer and a Gentleman* was my major movie star crush. I discovered from one of the multitude of PRs hovering around that he had not originally been placed next to me but on the same table as his then wife, Cindy Crawford, who was modelling in the shows. But because also at that table was a New York restaurateur Gere had some long-running issue with, he had swiftly been moved to avoid any unpleasantness. According to my diary of that evening, I pathetically failed to say anything other than hello to Gere or he to me, which is no doubt sad but true since I am always struck completely dumb in the company of anybody famous, let alone Richard Gere. All the same that does seem pretty dismal.

On my other side for that dinner was a Hollywood agent who said that he simply couldn't understand why Gere and Crawford were not sitting next to each other. I replied that surely people like to meet people if they go out to dinner, and suggested it's a bit dull to be put next to the person you arrive with. Wouldn't they like to meet somebody new and hopefully interesting? To which he looked horrified and replied, 'You have to understand they are only here to make an *appearance*. In my business we would do everything, EVERYTHING, to make their lives as pleasant as we can.'

It does not take much insight to deduce from this that, in his opinion, if you were Richard Gere, being seated next door to me would not achieve this target.

There was one other white shirt interlude in my life. I spent a summer wearing one in creamy linen, fitted close to the body with a lace collar. I almost always wore it with a black cotton skirt stitched in panels which flared to below the calf and a black leather belt with a silver buckle. Undoubtedly I had the famous Alfred Stieglitz images of his wife Georgia O'Keeffe in mind as an inspiration. It was an unusually hot summer and the sounds of reggae would drift all night through the windows of the flat in Ladbroke Grove, in west London, where I rented a room from a friend, and I was very much in love, of the anguished kind.

But that was in my 20s. After that my working life took over a greater part of my identity and somehow, as with the one I wore in the Gili shot, white shirts felt like wearing fancy dress, inhabiting the costume of a person I didn't even want to be – the impeccable professional.

Now I don't ever wear them. Probably because I realize, and sadly accept, that I never will live the life of the charismatic troubadour or beautiful desert artist, the people who I just might have thought I could be, when, in those earlier times, I put on a white shirt.

Lee Krasner's self-portrait as a young woman, 1928

13.

Aprons

In 1928 the 19-year-old Lee Krasner painted a figurative self-portrait. Krasner, who was to become one of America's leading abstract expressionists, chose to portray herself standing against a backdrop of trees working at a canvas, brushes and rag in hand and wearing an apron over a short-sleeved blue shirt. She stares intensely at us as we look at her. Her determination to be an artist is clear, though in 1928 aprons were still most often worn by women for domestic purposes rather than by ambitious Jewish girls hoping, as she was, to achieve a place at New York's National Academy of Design.

That apron was very similar to one that hangs on a rail in my kitchen. Mine falls to well below the knee in dun-coloured thick linen, and has a long tie which I wind round my waist and knot above the large central pocket. As I give it a satisfactory yank, it makes me feel somehow in control. The apron came from a very expensive French cooking shop, but as soon as I saw it I was in love and knew that it would be worth every penny. As it has been. It's been hanging there for years now, taken down most evenings when I cook supper, and almost always when people come and dine at the house, they will discover me wearing it to greet them. On a cost per wear it's probably the most economically efficient garment in the house.

My first cookbook was called *Floury Fingers* and it opens with the rhyme:

Floury Fingers,
Buttery Nose.
That's the way,
The Cooking Goes.

The introduction is illustrated by a line drawing of a small girl. Her pigtails are tied with bows and she stands at a kitchen counter with a huge mixing bowl, wearing an apron tied in a cross at the back. The text reads as follows:

This is your book.
I have made it
as easy as I can for you.
But there are one or two things
that are rather hard to do,
like 'knead' and 'sprinkle'.
Mummy will show you what to do.
It is rather hard
To beat up an egg with a fork.

Mummy will show you
how to do this as well.

In my case it was never Mummy who taught me to make the Tea-Party Scones, Jam Buns and Currant Biscuits, but my much-loved nanny, Janette, whose name is written in the front of the book, her 1962 Christmas present to me. She was an old-fashioned-style nanny with an aproned uniform who worked what now seems an unbelievable 24 hours, 6 days a week. We would follow the recipes together on the occasional afternoon, me in my own small cotton apron mimicking that of the girl in the illustration. The results of our baking were very often unsatisfactory. I recall rock-hard scones with burned currants being prised out from the metal cooking cases, although our sandwiches – cream cheese and jam – fared better. While this was going on 'Mummy' was at her office. She was never around at teatime. And neither was I for my son, when it came to my turn at maternity.

Still, the satisfaction in tying an apron and starting to cook has remained with me ever since. And although my first culinary experiences were under the tutelage of a nanny, it was my mother's dedication to good food that has stayed with me and my siblings. Let's be clear: our mother cooked regularly but she neither wore an apron

– which she thought of as 'too little housewifely' – nor did she bake sponges. She was and is a member of the generation that discovered good food via the writings of Elizabeth David, who brought a whole new joyful and sensual Mediterranean aesthetic to the provision of food, a business that had become so grim in ration-book post-war Britain. So we ate slow-cooked casseroles, tarragon-stuffed roast chickens, creamy boeuf stroganoffs, home-made mint sauce and always fresh vegetables. An enduring childhood memory is shucking peas and broad beans, delicious in its meditative repetitiveness and an activity I regard as a sign of summer arriving.

Aprons signify cooking and, no doubt because of her, cooking signifies home in my book. I don't cook because I enjoy it. I don't, like many people, find the process of chopping and stirring relaxing. Cooking is not for me a method of unwinding. I never look forward to cooking. But it roots me. There is something in the business of the very basic act of feeding people which, like the apron, provides a protective barrier so that what's happening elsewhere is less important during that time. The pressures of work and sometimes emotional stress temporarily retire behind it.

This kind of cooking is not about how adventurous or perfect or beautiful the food is. Others, who are what I call proper cooks, collect the very best ingredients, concentrate not only on taste but display, and view the meal more as one might view painting a picture rather than making a bed. My cooking is more on a subsistence level but even so it requires a degree of creation and preparation. Ordering in a takeaway or jamming a foil container in the oven does not hit the spot.

Aprons have always been symbols of domesticity and social status. Nowadays companies like Cath Kidston sell jaunty colourful aprons to the global middle class, and expensive homeware shops charge as much for a heavy linen apron as one might pay for a coat. But there was a time when the wearing of an apron was more charged. Infamously, Beau Nash, the 18th-century arbiter of taste, is supposed to have confronted the Duchess of Queensberry in the 1720s over her appearance at the Bath Assembly, where he was Master of Ceremonies, about her wearing a white apron. He told her she must remove it with the comment that 'none but Abigails appeared in white aprons', Abigail being a term for a lady's maid. The central issue here was that it was considered that the maintenance of the all-important social hierarchy relied upon differentiation of dress in class. What mayhem might result if duchesses thought it acceptable to dress in public like lady's maids? Even more worrying was the idea that the opposite might also be on the cards.

No, better to confine apron-wearing to the popular masquerades of the day, where wealthy women, rather than choosing to turn up at such parties in formal gowns, grabbed the opportunity to appear as rosy-cheeked, apron-clad milkmaids and shepherdesses. Aprons had become another element in the idealistic representation of country life that was popular in the art and literature of the time.

It has taken more than three centuries for the apron to move on and lose its stigma as an indicator of oppression – whether that be of class or gender. Now the bib top and straps of aprons are the stuff of fashion, while the real things are benefitting from the boom of interest in all things domestic. Instagrammers with nifty household cleaning tips are followed by millions and an inexhaustible supply of cookery books dominates the bestseller lists.

The idea of domestic activity may seem appealing as a counterpoint to the larger world, where so much is out of our control. Hours can be spent looking through feeds of professional tidiers who post videos showing how to fold T shirts and stack jeans, and who make guest appearances in the homeware departments of stores to help sell storage containers. Salvation can be found in a sparkling sink, contentment in a neatly ordered linen cupboard, achievement measured in a line of decoratively filled Kilner jars on a wooden shelf.

Even so, I doubt anybody could say in all honesty that they enjoy scrubbing the bath and vacuuming the stairs. Nor cleaning out the hair and scum of plugholes or hosing down the garbage bins. We like the bits that we can make look nice. Bring on the lavender-scented steam ironing and the sorting of a cutlery drawer, but when it comes to the real dirty work we would rather delegate it to someone else, if we can afford to.

Domestic objects might have become desirable but the hard slog remains something we usually avoid if we are in the position to. In other words, the question of who cleans up after us is still as much a denoter of social class as it ever was, despite any number of delightful aprons. Speaking of which, I never, ever, saw a single one of the army of cleaners, who would turn up every evening at the *Vogue* offices to wash our dirty coffee cups, empty the bins and clean the loos, wear anything even remotely resembling an apron.

Kate Moss in a slip dress at a 1995 awards evening

14

Slip Dresses

Slips slither. They are unintentional, precarious, sensual, eliding. And slip dresses are what I think of when I think of the story of my marriage.

Slips were originally underwear. Something to mitigate transparency; a light barrier between fabric and skin, suspended on slim straps and without any solid structure. They emerged from undercover in the early Nineties as a crucial part of the grunge armada, but their original appearance was on the Hollywood screen goddesses of the early Thirties. There, in pre-Hays Code days (the code that decreed what could and couldn't be seen on the American screen), the clinging, bias cut, body-exposing slip dress was a definer of glamour, paired with a peroxide wave, perhaps a fur stole and an attitude which said, 'Don't mess with me...Unless I want to be messed with.' Those slip dresses in satin and silk were not for the meek.

Following on from the Depression, the slip dress, along with the films of the time, was a mood lightener. It was a signifier of better days. It was unmitigated sex appeal. How completely opposite to the role slip dresses played when they returned to fashion, in 1993, as a rejection of exactly that immaculate, studied glamour.

Slip dresses were inescapably identified with the new cadre of fashion creatives who rose to fame at that time. The so-called British 'waif' models, Emma Balfour, Rosemary Ferguson and of course Kate Moss, wore slip dresses not only in fashion shoots but in real life; the new breed of Hollywood girls such as Sofia Coppola, Winona Ryder and Gwyneth Paltrow walked the red carpet in pared-down shimmering slivers; Carolyn Bessette married the closest thing the US had to a prince, John F Kennedy Jr, in an unadorned white slip, while a group of photographers with a more raw aesthetic were embraced by the mainstream. These photographers, including Mario Sorrenti, Nigel Shafran, Corinne Day and Juergen Teller, who had been working for smaller independent magazines, now found themselves working for magazines like *Vogue* and *Harper's Bazaar*.

Their defining point of view was to bring a new sense of reality to the careful construct that is fashion imagery. The issue of reality always begs the question: whose reality are we discussing here? Theirs was young and urban, featuring mattresses on bare wood floors, tenement windows, peeling plasterwork, all of which differentiated them from the plush Park Avenue duplexes and Mayfair ballrooms that were more traditionally associated with luxury and fashion. It was also very different to the image of the sassy, professional woman striding out onto the street, busily hailing cabs and going places, that had become a fixture of the previous yuppie fashion imagery.

Of course the clothes that were photographed were no less expensive than the clothes that had preceded them, but they looked unburdened by the weight of status and, as such, younger. While the shoots, even if they appeared carelessly tossed off, cost just as much as any shoots with their location scouts, film costs, retouching, hair and make-up, flights, catering, etc. Like slip dresses their attitude was casual, but, similarly, in their bare simplicity they demanded a different kind of perfection.

Slip dresses aren't the easiest of clothes to wear. They have no support for bosoms, they accentuate the swell of the stomach and, no matter how expensive, they are pretty unforgiving on the VPL front. But in their ease – just literally slip it on, no zips, no hooks, no buttons, over the head it goes – they can feel wonderful. Almost like wearing nothing at all. I bought many of mine from Ghost, where the founder Tanya Sarne had been working for years with a viscose material that had an element of bias stretch. I had them in navy, dark green, mustard, long and short.

Fashion is always to a certain extent about youth and the new, because in order to move things along it has to challenge what has come before. But in this short period of slip dress fame, 1993–4, the emphasis on youth in the fashion business was overwhelming. Everyone wanted to dress as if they were still at school. The then infamous, and now famous, Corinne Day shoot of Kate Moss wearing knickers, vests and T shirts, shot in a flat in Kensal Rise in north-west London, caused outrage in June 1993 when published in *Vogue*. For a magazine regarded as an arbiter and cheerleader for luxury and glamour, this was seen as a frightening endorsement of a nihilistic lifestyle – a rejection of traditional and acceptable aspiration.

Unbelievably to me, commentators across the globe weighed into the discussion and the pictures' publication became a worldwide news story. Susie Orbach, author of *Fat is a Feminist Issue*, described them as 'just this side of porn'. Others claimed they encouraged paedophilia. They were used as an illustration of what the US President Bill Clinton called 'heroin chic'. The *New York Times* ran an editorial on what they signified. The images are now held in museum collections.

When I first saw the pictures I thought they were beautiful and light and compelling. And that young women would recognize themselves in them. With her bony clavicles and slightly bandy legs, Kate Moss did not look like the push-up Wonderbra person of men's fantasy, but like someone playing around in a bedroom of a shared flat without any attempt at being a conventional sex object. In one she is wrapped in a grubby eiderdown, wearing a skimpy navy bra (actually from La Perla) and a pair of grey ankle socks. In another she is surrounded by the trailing wires of a cheap string of fairy lights, wearing, as the credits told us, a pair of 'lacy briefs, Warner's £10' and an Agnès B vest.

The editorial that opened the magazine that month suggests that:

> …*fashion appears to have deserted the sophisticated partygoer in favour of little girls lost with under-endowed chests, lank locks and blank looks. It also states that the single garment to update your wardrobe is a diaphanous dress, more Thirties than Seventies.*

That year I was 35, and although everyone had said how young I was to get the job at *Vogue*, I was not feeling young at all. I was Editor of the most important fashion magazine in the UK, which was also responsible for providing the lion's share of the money for the company.

Advertisers paid a large premium to feature in *Vogue*. Under my predecessors the sales figures of the magazine had been thought of as to some extent irrelevant, so long as the right people bought it – the right people being those who might buy the clothes. But when I and my colleague on the business side Stephen Quinn arrived at *Vogue*, times were changing.

My remit was unambiguously to sell more copies and reach a larger audience. It was no longer enough to sit back and relax on our reputation. There were new magazines on the newsstand, like *Marie Claire*, and all the national newspapers were launching fashion supplements. To run *Vogue* and increase the sales, particularly at a moment when the UK economy was in a downturn, was not the job of a schoolgirl, even if the current fashion suggested dressing like one.

In my private life I was by this stage going out with an American writer, Paul Spike. The year that suddenly *Vogue* was filled with supermodels photographed barefoot, seemingly bare-faced, in ankle-length slips with urchin haircuts, was a difficult one for our relationship. We had been together for a few years, on and off. During that period we had broken up and got back together so many times that I think both of us had lost track of what we wanted. We were sad and uncertain when we were apart, but we weren't happy, in the way that we probably both knew we should be, when we were together. We loved each other, but that didn't mean to say we were suited to each other. What I did know was that I wanted a child. And what Paul knew was that he didn't want another child – he already had a much-loved two.

On the weekends I'd put on one of my slip dresses and we would take his children, Matthew and Emma, to one of the London parks for picnics or to a local Chinese for dinner. I would try, usually successfully, to forget about my work at *Vogue* and concentrate on the business of being his girlfriend.

Throughout my life I have never defined myself as an executive career woman. Nor was it how I wanted to be seen by others. That was no doubt a reason for choosing the informal clothes I wore much of the time, but it's a great deal more complicated to analyse why I so deliberately steered clear of being viewed in that light. After all, many women then and now want to be successful outside the parameters of the home and family. Being Editor of *Vogue* was taking on a very public job which I knew would be defining, and there was a large part of me that was struggling with that.

While I loved my work and was honoured to have been given a chance to do the job, I was increasingly worried that all around me my friends were getting married and having children. Every week another member of staff would come in to my office, close the door and say they had something they had to tell me – they were pregnant. With each announcement I heard the noisy, frightening ticking of that clock – Tick, Tock, Tick, Tock – which no amount of career success could silence.

In fact, I was worried that professional success might be a positive disadvantage in my relationships with men. That the part of me that was successful at work was a disincentive to someone wanting to be with me. Wouldn't somebody who had not known me before all of this, before I had this almost public role, view me as officious, controlling and too high profile?

So at this point, not defining myself as the *Vogue* Editor seemed important to my and Paul's relationship. Being able to slope around in a slip dress was part of that. He was a freelance writer, sometimes successfully and lucratively employed, and at other times not. He was supportive of me in my work but would also get angry if he felt he wasn't being paid due attention in his own right. Not as the plus one of the Editor of *Vogue*.

Along with the job came a certain amount of business entertaining – because that is what ultimately these evenings are, even if it was something as impressive as throwing a dinner for the BAFTA awards or dining with Gianni Versace when he came to town. On those evenings I would not be wearing a slip dress but would get into my kit – more likely a structured velvet cocktail dress by British designers like Antony Price and Tomasz Starzewski – and Paul would get into his suit and an Hermès tie, and I would pray that the seating plan would not place him on a table somewhere near the door while I was seated that much closer to God (whoever God was that night).

In April 1994 we broke up again, and Paul moved out of the flat we shared. I was panicking that, if Paul and I weren't going to ultimately work out, I would be leaving it too late for me to find anyone else and have a child with them. He hated me thinking like that, as if a child was the only reason I would want to be with him, and he was also dealing with demons of his own. Once again we were miserable without each other, and one evening a few weeks later he came to see me in the shared flat he had moved out of, carrying a diamond ring and with a date booked at Chelsea register office – three days away. He said he realized that all he wanted was to marry me and have our children. It was make-my-mind-up time. And it took me absolutely no time at all to decide to take the risk and go ahead and marry him.

We told no one other than my sister, Nicky, and brother-in-law, Con, who we asked to be witnesses. I bought a white Ghost dress, not a slip dress for this occasion but a calf-length embroidered V neck with long sleeves, and a white, heavily embroidered Dries van Noten shawl to wear with it. On the morning of our wedding I went to the hairdresser. The boy who washed my hair asked if it was for a special occasion. 'Yes,' I answered, 'it's for a wedding.' He replied that this weekend he was going to his mother's wedding in Broadstairs. She was marrying his best friend. 'Broadstairs is funny that way. We're such a close community,' he told me. So secret were we keeping it that I hadn't wanted to tell him that it was me who was getting married.

The dress was a little transparent, which I didn't think appropriate for a marriage ceremony, so on the way from the hairdresser to the office, where I planned to spend most of the morning pre-wedding (because, given it was a secret, what else was I going to do), I dropped into Fenwick's near the office to try and find a slip to wear under it. They were all the wrong shape or the wrong colour or had straps you could see through the dress. So instead I bought a pair of white Spanx which were uncomfortable and which I instantly regretted, but was now stuck with, as at least they had decency on their side.

Nicky produced small lily-of-the-valley buttonholes for the men and a bridal posy for me. When we arrived at the register office we were asked whether we wanted the large or small room. Answer, small (there were only the four of us). And during the ceremony I kept wondering when I would realize what was truly happening, rather than watching it happen to someone else. After the wedding we had lunch at San Lorenzo where, fortified by champagne, I called my parents from the phone in the hallway outside the loos to break the news. 'Are you crazy?' was my father's response.

A month later my parents hosted a wedding party for us. I had more time to find something to wear and chose a navy chiffon Valentino slip dress with tiny straps and a fringed hem. Then we took Matthew and Emma on a summer holiday to Deià in Majorca instead of going on a honeymoon. On our return I discovered, joyfully, that I was pregnant.

*1620 Marcus Gheeraerts portrait of a pregnant woman,
part of a short-lived vogue for the pregnancy portrait*

15.

Maternity Clothes

During my years at *Vogue* I was scarcely ever interviewed without a reference being made to my weight. Headlines like 'Meet the *Vogue* Editor who's size 14 – and happy' loomed loudly over whatever else I might have to say. What always struck me as strange about this was that the women (and it was almost always women who wrote these pieces) who were interviewing me would generally take the view that our obsession with being thin (both as a society and as reflected in *Vogue*) was misplaced. But they still considered it worth pointing out my clothes size.

I can't say it bothered me at all. I have always thought that if you are a figure with a public profile you have to put up with a commentary about your appearance, although I have been intrigued by the fact that my successor Edward Enninful does not, as a man, seem to have any observations about his appearance written about him, and definitely not about what he might weigh. It was, though, one of the many reasons why I was so thrilled to be pregnant. Hurrah, a pink ticket to be fat. A period when I could be excused, at least partially, from the tyranny of appearance.

Retrospectively, I realized that the unusually tired and faintly nauseous moments I had on the family holiday in Deià that we took soon after our wedding were clearly signs that I was pregnant. At the time the thought didn't cross my mind, and I cavalierly tucked into copious carafes of white wine and shared long evenings with the couple next door, the fashion designer Edina Ronay and her husband/business partner, photographer Dick Polak. They, like us, had rented a small stone, terraced house and on that holiday they became and have remained very good friends.

They also had their two teenage children with them and I admired Edina's apparent ability to achieve the enviable combination of parenting while living the life of a golden hippie – rising late to shimmy around in a lime green slip dress, hitting the beach as the sun started to sink. In contrast, I was feeling heavy and slow. I put it down to the aftermath of our unexpected wedding and being exhausted by work. But I remember wishing that I felt more glamorous and casual and generally better on this, my first holiday as a married woman.

Photographs of that trip show me mainly dressed in oversized shirts and not looking anything like as appealing as my next-door neighbour. As a recently married step-parent I still wasn't at all sure what kind of parenting I was supposed to do, and took Paul's lead with Matthew and Emma, who were entering the less amenable stage of teenagedom. I was deeply fond of them and their addition to my life has been nothing but a plus. But even so there were good-tempered and bad-tempered days, and I know that I was hoping desperately that I would soon have my own child to join us on such holidays.

On our return, from the moment I spotted that confirming blue dot on the pregnancy stick, I embraced the physical sensations of pregnancy, in particular the gain in weight. By the time I had my first scan I was already a substantial size. None of that 'but where have you hidden the baby?' stuff for me. When people saw me they couldn't have missed the swollen breasts, limbs and faintly placid face. The baby might still have only been the size of a passion fruit but I was already lumbering around cautiously, worried that any bump or knock would damage my precious cargo.

At work I was trying to figure out how to dress in a role where what I wore was part of the job. Had I not been the Editor I would have simply thrown myself into huge smocks for eight months, but that didn't seem to be the right attitude, especially since I was surrounded by many other women who managed to carry off their pregnancies in great style, scarcely altering their mode of dress. Several of my fashion editors had produced two or three babies while managing to travel around the world on fashion shoots without looking like a hippo. In my job I knew I was meant to be a person who had cracked the issue of pregnancy style, but that was far from the case.

Bear in mind that the fashion of the moment had begun to reboot and was moving towards something more high voltage and streamlined after the deliberate downbeat of grunge. The cover of the 1994 *Vogue* September issue, published as I returned from that holiday, was a headshot of model Nadja Auermann, a chillingly beautiful peroxide Valkyrie, photographed in glamorous, ring-flash mode by Nick Knight. Referencing the work of Seventies photographers like Guy Bourdin and Helmut Newton, the picture was electric, her white hair contrasted with a pair of impenetrable dark glasses, glittering pale pink lipstick and a sliver of a crushed red velvet dress. It was a statement of intent that the magazine was embracing a more high fashion, hard-edged chic. Neon colours, slick leathers, tight, swathed body-con minis. Everything that was in complete contrast to how at that time I wanted to dress myself. I craved soft fabrics and gentle shades, clothes that seemed to encourage compromise rather than confrontation and that would protect me

YOU magazine shoot when I was pregnant, spring 1995

and the embryo, but in a completely different way to the glossy armour of a professional woman.

There was a maternity clothes shop near the office which sold skirts with thick elasticated waistbands that stretched over the bump while the rest of the skirt was a traditional pencil shape. I bought several, despite the fact that the fashion team considered them unspeakably dowdy. A *Mail on Sunday YOU* magazine shoot about how a *Vogue* Editor dresses in pregnancy shows me squeezed into the black lace skin of a cocktail dress by the London designer Ben de Lisi, which I wore to almost every party

I went to for the whole of that winter. In another picture I am there in another of his designs, a crimson velvet devoré smock worn over one of those skirts with thick tights.

Neither outfit made any effort to disguise my pregnant body, a body I was delighted to hand over to this baby growing inside my womb. But I was surprised at the changes. The 'bump' is one thing, but the way that our breasts become an extension of that mound as the waist is swallowed up, the way limbs and ankles thicken, and the fact that it is not only your stomach but your back that expands, were unexpected, and made demands of my clothing that I hadn't anticipated. Swelling feet made wearing the high heels I relied upon to give me some stature (in various ways) more uncomfortable, as well as made me nervous that I might trip and fall.

How we feel about the appearance of pregnancy is so personal. For every woman like myself who wants to shout out through their dress that they are carrying a child, there are those who prefer to keep themselves looking as much like the selves they had previously been for as long as possible. Having this choice, though, is a relatively recent luxury. It was only 50 years ago that the Pregnancy Discrimination Act came into force, making it illegal for a woman to lose her job because she was pregnant. And even now the issue of pregnancy and employment remains unresolved.

Only the other day a young woman asked me whether she should tell a prospective employer that she was hoping to become pregnant soon and was on a course of IVF. I advised her to keep it to herself. It is such a personal matter, and emotional enough without it being part of a job interview. And, in all honesty, despite any number of HR rulings, few employers are entirely thrilled by the idea of hiring somebody who will shortly be taking maternity leave. The world needs mothers, but pregnancy is an inconvenience in the workplace.

So, for very many years, women tried as hard as they could not to appear pregnant. Certainly there were no clothes available specifically for the period of pregnancy. Curiously it was in the mid-1800s that something called a maternity corset came into existence, designed to disguise the fact of pregnancy. What a strange development at this time when Victoria, the monarch of the day, was rarely not herself pregnant, and therefore you might have expected her to be in favour of exposing that condition. But no. The opposite was the case.

For over a century more, dressing for pregnancy continued in reality to be dressing to disguise pregnancy. In the Thirties and Forties pregnant women were advised to wear dresses patterned with polka dots and florals or with large bows and ruffles on the front, which supposedly made their condition less obvious. The maternity smock, often worn with a neat skirt or narrow slacks, was popular – a particularly hideous garment with voluminous sleeves and prim neat collar, as if to make it as clear as possible that the pregnancy had nothing to do with naked bodies or sex.

In 1956 my mother co-authored a book called *Lady Behave: A Guide to Modern Manners*. Under the heading Baby on the Way, the authors write, 'The modern working mother-to-be has an easier path than the girl we remember who worked in a newspaper office…she used to appear with a large satin bow on top of what she used to describe as her "indigestion".' The chapter doesn't actually advise on what should be worn, restricting itself to saying '…since girls go around so much more socially, they make a point of wearing clothes that do not obviously proclaim maternity, even to wearing slacks or jeans…And the modern young men seem glad to take them around.' To put this into some context, on the previous page is an outline of what to wear For a Two Week Mediterranean Cruise. It recommends: a beach coat, a stole (to wear with dance dresses on deck), a full petticoat and two sunbathing outfits (shorts, bra and jacket), among other items on a very long list.

That phrase 'do not obviously proclaim maternity' is at the heart of the matter. Times have changed from when the condition was something to be hidden. A generation of celebrities used to sharing their lives on social media have helped that along. Kim Kardashian twice looked gloriously and unashamedly pregnant wearing a vast range of stretchy tubes as much in the public eye as ever. Beyoncé broke the news of her pregnancy with twins by posting a picture on Instagram of herself as a Jeff Koons-style Madonna, wearing only a brown bra and a long white veil against a backdrop of garish flowers, her enlarged bare stomach centre stage. The Duchess of Sussex, once her pregnancy was announced, was rarely seen in public without placing a protective hand on her stomach which couldn't fail but draw attention to her status.

Yet at the same time we have an admiration for those whose pregnancy is contained and controlled. We envy women who have a small 'neat' bump. Whose growing baby seems to have hidden themselves in some previously unknown cavity in the body, only appearing in the latest trimester. Who throughout the entire, very physical process of carrying a child appear immune to the indignities of the condition: heartburn, flatulence, hormonal craziness, bloating and emotional vulnerability.

So it's not surprising, even if not desirable, that now pregnancy has turned into yet another fashion opportunity. It's a way to maintain an element of control, to own it, rather than have it own you.

In my beaded skirt with French Connection's Stephen Marks
at Vogue's *'Best of British' party, 1998*

16.

The Beaded Skirt

In 1998 British fashion was having one of its hoopla moments. Cresting on the wave of Cool Britannia and the optimism of Tony Blair and his new Labour government, there was a raft of colourful, eclectic and imaginative designers who had emerged after the recession of the early days of the decade. Alexander McQueen, Antonio Berardi, Matthew Williamson, Clements Ribeiro, Hussein Chalayan, Stella McCartney, et al., were drawing international fashion press and buyers to London in growing numbers.

The husband and wife team of Suzanne Clements and Inacio Ribeiro had designed and given me a skirt they called the Alex. It was crocheted in silky magenta thread with starbursts of a dark flame beading. At their catwalk show it was worn with bare skin beneath. Mine had a more modest white slip.

That June, *Vogue* published a 'Best of British' edition of the magazine. The cover was a headshot of Kate Moss, photographed by Nick Knight – just her beautiful face staring out at you with that mixture of challenge and submission that is uniquely hers. Who were the Best of

British of that time? Couple-of-the-moment, gallerist Jay Jopling and his wife, artist Sam Taylor-Wood (now Taylor-Johnson); the World Cup England squad's footballers Tony Adams, Teddy Sheringham and Alan Shearer (photographed in plain white T shirts to avoid any sponsorship conflicts of interest); Chris Evans, who was then presenting *TFI Friday*; Ewan McGregor in his glam rock metallic *Velvet Goldmine* costume; and Christopher Lloyd's garden at Great Dixter, with his famed red hot pokers standing to attention.

We installed the photographer David Bailey in a tent outside the Natural History Museum to shoot the denizens of London Fashion Week between shows – models like Karen Elson and Erin O'Connor, established designers Betty Jackson, Nicole Farhi, Manolo Blahnik, and industry creatives like hairstylist Sam McKnight and make-up artist Pat McGrath. And incongruously, but rather fabulously, the issue also included Peter Mandelson, the Honourable Member for Hartlepool, photographed by Snowdon lounging at home on an Eames chair, red boxes by his side, under a portrait of Cromwell.

All in all it was a time when the world, or anyway our London world, seemed to be going in the right direction. The Good Friday Agreement had been signed and approved with a huge majority in a referendum, and we didn't yet know that England's performance in the World Cup would end insalubriously with a fatal tantrum by David Beckham, leading to him being sent off.

The magazine held a party to celebrate the 'Best of British' issue in a courtyard and warehouse space owned by the Lisson Gallery, just off the Edgware Road. In those days magazines were still hosting parties for no reason other than to celebrate themselves, without having to promote or advertise a brand that was footing the bill. Despite the British theme we decided to style the gritty urban spot as the courtyard of a Moroccan riad, filling the concrete floors and paved paths with bright geraniums and blue hydrangeas, candlelit lanterns, low benches and cyclamen cushions.

And I wore that Clements Ribeiro skirt, a skirt that I still love for the way it made me feel that night. For unlike many of the nights that I hosted parties for *Vogue*, that night was one I felt I owned. It was a reflection of the way I wanted my *Vogue* to be – insouciant, British, cultured, not ostentatious, but also exceptional.

There is an intriguing and accurate theory advanced by the late writer Angela Carter, in an essay she wrote for the magazine several years earlier, that style turns on the hinge of a decade. That we start a decade existing within a certain dominant style, pivoting towards another somewhere in the middle. By 1998 we had moved again into a more sumptuous and luxurious era, having travelled from the tag end of the power-dressed Eighties, where the decade began, through periods of grunge and restrained minimalism.

Liam Gallagher drifted in with Patsy Kensit, who wore the mandatory white slip dress of that time. Kate Moss was there with a posse in what could have been a Moroccan velvet smock. Martha Stewart (how on earth did she come to be there?) posed for pictures in a baby blue satin jacket. Cath Kidston and Helen Fielding both arrived in pink cardigans. Although it was May, the weather was exceptionally balmy, creating a rare occasion when the temperature matched the enchanting evening light that time of year brings.

That skirt currently hangs in a cupboard in our spare bedroom, between a vintage emerald satin opera coat and a pillar box red velvet duvet of a jacket. Occasionally it graduates into the wardrobe where I keep the clothes I am actually wearing, in the hope I might slip into it again. I haven't worn it in years, yet I look at it often, shimmying on the hanger with the gaiety of a bright young thing. And I remember that evening and how happy I was.

I left the party to have dinner at Le Caprice with a man I had met only a few days previously at the opening of an exhibition of Anish Kapoor's work at the Hayward Gallery. Two months before, my husband had moved out of our home and our marriage was in terrible shape. Mr Caprice was not, it turned out, going to be the solution. But for that night, in my Clements Ribeiro skirt that rattled like a soft wind when I walked, it seemed like he just might be.

The trench, Rihanna style, 2018

17.

Trench Coats

My favourite coat, no contest, in all my years at *Vogue*, was a trench. Not your classic khaki waterproof, but a smoke grey, cashmere Lanvin trench. It was soft and warm, with a tie belt that you could knot into a satisfactory waist, and it was Lanvin, for God's sake. At that point in time, at the turn of the millennium, Lanvin was one of those stealth-style labels that quietly shrieked (and such contradictions do exist quite happily in fashion), 'I am a person in the know'. It was a label that said that although you could afford to, you had no need to show off your wealth. Or not in an ostentatious way. Though, of course, that you were wearing Lanvin, with its easy silhouette, black grosgrain trims and wildly expensive fabrics, was obvious to anybody who knew their fashion.

I wore that trench to years of shows. It kept me warm when we were seated in some icy warehouse on the Parisian Périphérique better suited to Scandi noir than a set for a luxury fashion show. It was reassuringly cosy and made me feel a fraction safer when I wore it to fly home from Milan, when the plane – packed with other journalists, stylists, make-up artists, buyers – would take off from Linate airport and, as it climbed over the Alps, often begin to shake. On so many journeys, headphones clamped into my ears and offering every kind of deal to the gods of fortune if the plane would only land safely, I would wrap the fabric more closely around me. I would think how often I had worn the same coat, felt the same fears and arrived home. How a coat can make you feel safer is a real example of matter over mind.

A trench coat, that somewhat anonymous, seemingly practical piece of clothing, held no allure for me until then, in my late 30s. If I thought of trenches at all previously, and I don't remember having done so, I would have considered them coats for people who, unlike myself, were engaged in some kind of 'business'. Such was the way I thought in my teens, 20s and early 30s, when 'business' was another world. Before the point when I accepted that the job I was doing was definitely business too.

No. Business was something that had attracted those of my contemporaries who had gone into established professions straight from university – banking, law, insurance, corporate finance – and who had been able to buy their own flats and own a car and earned a lot more than I did a great deal quicker. Those were the people who might have worn a trench.

But then came that moment in the Nineties when the whole trench shebang changed and that beige coat, devoid of any charm that I could identify, underwent a transformation. Burberry, a company that had been consigned to the doldrums of the duty-free franchises, languishing in the domain of time-poor execs with a cancelled flight to Singapore, was given a clever makeover. And the trench, that unlikely saviour of a fashion company, was designated the spine of the business. By polishing up an item that at root had both purpose and heritage, the clever folks at Burberry revived the fortunes not only of the company but also of the coat that they had invented as military wear in the early part of the 20th century. So successful were they that it became, against all odds, tremendously fashionable.

The early trench (more of a jacket than a coat) was originally only worn by the officer class and began life as a hybrid that combined the appeal of clothes for upper class outdoor life with the functional aspects of clothes for war. It was a more practical and a lighter alternative to the previous heavy serge greatcoats, had epaulettes at the shoulder for military decorations, a buckled belt that gathered the volume of fabric, straps at the wrist to prevent rain leaking in and large flapped pockets for maps and other essentials.

It's hard to imagine that anyone predicting the future trajectory of any item could envisage it surviving the slaughterhouse that was the trenches of First World War to emerge a century later as a barely bottom-scraping mini coat worn by celebrities like Rihanna. Could anyone have imagined that a piece of clothing specifically designed to withstand the blood, muck and excrement of the battlefield would be a favourite now worn by style royalty, from Catherine Deneuve to Olivia Palermo?

Part of the secret of the trench's success is a sphinx quality. It doesn't shriek gender or sexuality. It is quietly strong with a somewhat enigmatic appeal. For this reason, in the old days of Hollywood, costume designers often viewed it as shorthand for independent, go-getting women, like those played by Katharine Hepburn, Ingrid Bergman, Marlene Dietrich. And for men it quickly became the standard costume for private eyes and undercover agents – think Humphrey Bogart.

And it's that somewhat unspecific element that makes it a useful tool in fashion portraiture. Anyone of any age can wear a trench. It's neuter. A hardy perennial of Ageless Style roundups – in your 50s you can, we learn, always wear navy, a white shirt and a trench. It was also frequently called in as a fail-safe shoot option when the subject was a size 14 or above. Although that wasn't the case with the most famous trench picture of my era – the cover portrait of the Duchess of Cambridge by the photographer Josh Olins for the 100th anniversary issue of British *Vogue*.

From the very start of the conversation about her *Vogue* shoot, the duchess had wanted to be dressed in an everyday manner. There were to be no ballgowns and diamonds. She wanted off-duty portraits rather than the costume of formal wear. So instead the *Vogue* team arrived at the shoot in a cottage on the Sandringham Estate with rails of denim, farm-style shirts and, yes, trench coats, pulled together by the fashion director Lucinda Chambers. It was a freezing January day when the sun was low in the sky over fields of frost, and our royal subject gamely posed in thin Breton tops and cotton shirts until, by early afternoon, the temperature was becoming brutal.

We were all keen to get as many pictures as possible, and things had been going well. So with the dropping temperatures in mind, we all agreed to try one more for inside the magazine, one with her wearing a narrow-shouldered, brown suede Burberry trench coat and wheeling a bike. Our magazine was to celebrate the centenary of *Vogue* and would be published in May, so I didn't really think it likely we would feature a dark coat on the cover at that time of year. When the duchess emerged from the cottage where she was changing, Lucinda had also put her in a hat I wasn't crazy about, but since I had thought we already had the cover in the bag, I wasn't too worried, if Catherine was happy.

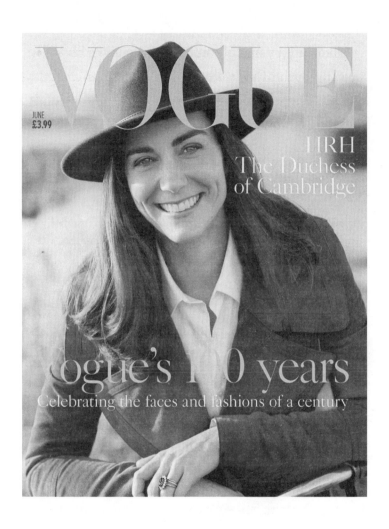

Centenary cover of British Vogue *by Josh Olins, June 2016*

The image I thought would work for a cover showed her wearing a pair of wide-legged, high-waisted jeans and a checked shirt with gilt buttons – hair loose, eyes narrowed slightly, as she looked into the sun and walked through a field of long grass. It had a golden aura. If you hadn't known who she was, it could have been shot on a prairie and she the healthy, homespun heroine in times of bounty.

But through the process that is involved in a partnership between a fashion magazine, the National Portrait Gallery, a photographer and a member of the royal family, a decision that at first had seemed pretty straightforward became more convoluted. We all had different points of view and as we all looked again and again at the images, we found it hard to agree on exactly which shot should be the cover.

The duchess didn't like the one that I first favoured and the photographer, Josh, didn't like another option. So in the way that so often happens in these things, through a process of negotiation and compromise, an outsider raced up to win. Six months after this shoot, there she was – smiling out of the magazine as she leaned on the handlebars of the bike, wearing that coat over a crisp white shirt, unaffected and natural, a country girl with an enormous sapphire engagement ring. Consort of our future King – in a trench.

18

The Geography Teacher's Dress

When low-rise skinny jeans and ballerina flats and huge bags hoved into view on city streets, somewhere around the turn of the millennium, I instead spent a lot of time in pretty dresses with V necks, fitted waists and gently flared skirts that floated around the knee.

I call them Geography teacher's dresses, which is odd, because the teacher that inspired this term was not a Geography teacher but one of my English teachers at school. She often wore mid-length floral dresses in garish yellows or reds, with a low neck that showed off her suntanned but faintly crepey skin (though now I realize she may not even have reached 40), and she was the teacher who told my parents, after they had queued up at a parent-teacher evening for her opinion on my next steps, that perhaps I should consider teaching in a kindergarten. There is nothing at all wrong with teaching in a kindergarten, but anybody who knew my parents or my highly academic school or indeed the teacher would also have known that this recommendation was not intended as a compliment.

But that was decades before my own embrace of Geography teacher's dresses. When I could not have known that I would become a semi-single mother living in a terraced house in north-west London with a stepdaughter, a young son and a nanny. And when I clearly could not, and certainly did not, predict that I would become Editor of *Vogue*. It was years before I would value a dress for the fact that it was easy to run down the street wearing it when you needed to chase after a small child who was hurtling themselves in the direction of an oncoming lorry. Or made it easy to crouch down to kiss a grazed knee better. Or allow lolling around on the grass in the park with cartons of juice and baby wipes without feeling you were in any danger of flashing your knickers.

One of the first times my son, Sam, commented on my appearance was when I was wearing such a dress. It was in a pale pink silky fabric with small white flowers and he looked at me as I dressed one morning and casually said I looked nice. He was about five. When I arrived at work I noticed male colleagues too complimented me on the dress, clearly liking such a pretty, undemanding and unconfrontational piece of clothing.

Pretty is an intriguing word. According to the *Shorter Oxford English Dictionary*, it has a range of meanings. It can be 'beautiful in a slight, dainty or diminutive way... Pleasing to the eye, the ear or the aesthetic sense'. But in its earliest form it was also used as a faintly pejorative term for 'cunning, crafty, capricious, artful'. In other words, not entirely trustworthy and certainly insubstantial. One letter away from petty. Which you could successfully argue is how pretty is often viewed in art and fashion.

During my years at *Vogue* it was clear that calling something pretty – dresses, models, photographs – was a term of thinly veiled contempt. Pretty was too immediate, too crowd-pleasing, not challenging enough to be regarded as inspiring and directional, which is what high fashion is intended to be.

As someone who came to the fashion business relatively late, this suspicion of prettiness was not my personal opinion, even though I understood why it existed. Should a fashion picture feature clothes most people would consider conventionally pretty, more often than not the fashion editor would throw a curveball, swerving it away from something simply good-looking into something that would provoke a deeper reaction from the viewer: 'Why is that there? Why is that happening?' It could be a blue Afro wig or flower-pot hat, circus make-up or sometimes something very simple like a pair of shoes that looked utterly out of kilter with pretty clothes, therefore causing you to look again.

It was similar to the attitude that deemed the most admired designers in the industry were usually those that in some manner subverted convention; be that the repurposed historical references of Vivienne Westwood, John Galliano or Alexander McQueen, the deconstructed shapes of Japanese designers or the dour but compelling androgyny of the Belgium school such as Ann Demeulemeester and Raf Simons.

Editing British *Vogue* was a continual tightrope act between pleasing the constituency who would value fashion for this kind of originality and extraordinariness and those who wanted to find ideas and clothes in the magazine that they could wear. Other of the international *Vogue*s were likely to focus more on the first group and gain acclaim for the challenges of their imagery. But by catering as much as I chose to for the second, more mainstream group, my *Vogue* didn't garner that particular kudos.

However, one of the most exciting aspects of being a *Vogue* Editor is that you can create the magazine that you want, and I wanted mine to be beautiful and accessible and relevant. I always had in mind, when I was making decisions, a woman who commuted daily from the Home Counties, who didn't earn a huge amount, but who would buy *Vogue* at Waterloo station on payday as her treat for the weekend. She would not be reading *Vogue* bought on office expenses, as of course many industry subscribers did, and she might on any Friday choose instead to buy another magazine, *Elle* or *Glamour* or *Tatler*, for her indulgence. I had to earn her pounds and I derived a real satisfaction from knowing that my vision was successful, increasing circulation and ultimately making over 200 million pounds profit for Condé Nast over my tenure. I never minded that much about the people who didn't like it. Nor about the people who found it odd that I was a *Vogue* Editor who would choose to go about her day in a pretty, but insipid and unfashionable Geography teacher's dress.

Halle Berry in Juicy Couture, 2003

19.

Track Suits

Just after the turn of the millennium there was a thing for Juicy Couture velour track suits. Juicy Couture was started in 1995 by Gela Nash (later to marry Duran Duran's John Taylor) and Pamela Skaist-Levy, two doll-sized, long-haired Californian women who had the clever idea of reviving an item from the Seventies that was then, almost exclusively, worn as sports or after-sports wear. They took the trackie, reworked it in velour (and the cosseting but slightly naff velour is the essential element here), produced it in a range of sweetie colours, splashed a faux heraldry-inspired logo on it and gave it a brand name that was perfect for the age. Gela and Pamela had the intuition to see that the downbeat-style mood of the early Nineties would be eclipsed by the pendulum swinging in the completely opposite direction towards a full-on-bling, logo-laden time of ostentatious consumption. Juicy Couture – perfectly, indulgently expensive sounding.

Juicy was a Los Angeles native encapsulating the dress-down vibe of the city. Paris Hilton, Madonna, Jennifer Lopez, Britney Spears – these were the papped celebrities of the moment, constantly photographed on Rodeo Drive and at LA arrivals with their giant tote bags, oversized sunnies, stripy bleached hair and their track suits. The brand's eye-catching brassiness was an ideal addition to celeb style. The sloppiness inherent in a velour track suit made it the perfect foil for those days, when there was no such thing as too many logos, too deep a fake tan, too many handbags. No such thing as too much – period.

As rap and hip-hop went mainstream, track suits referenced popular street culture, but given the Juicy touch they also had the ideal degree of you-just-have-to-unzip-me-sexiness that was part of the appeal of girl bands like Destiny's Child and All Saints. Yes we do Girl Power. But we're also hot. No wonder Juicy rip-offs flooded the high street and became a staple of nights in, watching the newly launched *Big Brother*, as well as raucous hen parties, which were enjoying a burgeoning popularity. Less predictable was that their startling popularity and the massive increase in fashion consumerism they epitomized straddled pre- and post-9/11.

The world changed irrevocably on the day we watched two planes fly out of a clear blue sky into New York's Twin Towers. Everyone remembers where they were at the time. I was on holiday in a beautiful house belonging to the Duke of Wellington that overlooked the plain of Granada. I was a guest of his daughter, the writer Jane

Wellesley, part of a group that included the *Bridget Jones* author Helen Fielding, the poet Mick Imlah and the foreign correspondent Marie Colvin.

I had been taking a post-lunch siesta when Mick Imlah rushed into my bedroom with the words 'there's big news breaking from New York'. I rushed downstairs to the basement, which housed the only television in the house, a small black-and-white TV, in a room beside the kitchen. We, the house's guests and staff, crowded round to watch the horrifying images in grainy monochrome on repeat, accompanied by a Spanish commentary that most of us couldn't understand. Marie, *The Sunday Times* expert on Middle-Eastern politics, immediately guessed it was the work of Bin Laden, a name that most of us at that stage knew nothing of. Suddenly, the world seemed terrifying. The skies potentially housing untold numbers of such weapons for jihadi terrorists. The certainties of the morning spent basking round the pool were dashed to pieces and replaced by a real yet unspecified fear.

Very unusually, this was a holiday where I had left Sam at home with his nanny, Kirsty, and I was desperate to speak to him – far less to check that he was OK, than, as so often has been the case, to make myself feel safe by hearing his voice. When I called he was blissfully unaware of what had happened and, instead, was focused on the fact that although the boys were meant to sit next to the girls in his new class, there were too many boys so some of them got to sit with each other. Not him though. He had the bad luck to have been paired with a girl – Alba. I commiserated with this unfortunate state of affairs, but reminded him how great Alba was, and then told Kirsty not to let him anywhere near the television as I didn't want the images of people jumping from the burning skyscrapers to enter his mind.

Within days the US-led coalition began the march to war. Yet for all that world-altering turmoil, branded luxury continued its inexorable rise. New brands, new stores, new designers proliferated. And so did the popularity of the velour track suit. At *Vogue* we talked about how we slobbed out in them when we got home after work, particularly those, and there were many, who were battling with post-pregnancy tummies. More surprisingly, movie and TV stars still paraded in them – Mariah Carey, Catherine Zeta-Jones, Eva Longoria – their popularity undaunted by the cheaper roll-out.

I was wearing a Juicy Couture track suit a couple of years later, on the evening that David and I began our romance. Knowing what I know now, which is how deeply unattractive he finds my wearing elastic-waisted, baggy trousers, it is remarkable that the relationship ever began.

He was a friend of more than 20 years who I had invited to stay for the weekend in a Devon barn I was borrowing from friends. My father had died earlier that year and my mother was with us. I thought David would provide some intelligent company to converse with when the rest of us there were looking after small kids.

I had no thought of a different kind of relationship with him, but perhaps somewhere I did, as I do remember thinking at some point in the early evening that at least I had a suntan, which might make the track suit look more appealing.

When I told him recently I was writing about wearing a track suit that evening, I hadn't expected him to remember, but he answered, 'Yes. Wasn't it white – or a kind of cream?' I find it impossible now to imagine that I could ever have owned a white velour track suit, but deep in the recesses of my memory I have a very, very vague feeling he could have been right. Which to my mind makes it even more extraordinary. What could ever have possessed me to buy a white velour track suit?

Wearing my perfect dress to give a talk in Kiev, 2019

20.

The Perfect Dress

While writing this book I have found the perfect dress. It is from the Indian designer Saloni and is in multicoloured checked crepe de Chine, mid-calf, with a cuffed elbow-length sleeve, a shirt collar and tiny metal buttons down the front. The colours are joyous in the same way that, as a child, a new packet of colourful pens always were. It is narrow enough above the waist to give me some shape but floats in a satisfactory way over my stomach and hips. It is a marvel.

It is of course *my* perfect dress and not *the* perfect dress. During the *Vogue* years I was always publishing pictures captioned the 'perfect' this and the 'perfect' that. Perfect is such a winning word. But by definition, it is also wildly imprecise and totally inaccurate. You could go as far as saying it is a lie. Perfection is only in the eye of the beholder or the person who is making that value judgement. As a reality it is surely nonexistent. So that perfect dress – my perfect dress – like all the perfect dresses, jackets, bags, shirts and trousers, is only perfect to the person who deems it thus. My perfect dress is highly likely to be nothing like yours. You might well think it's hideous. But you probably wouldn't, since when I collected it from the local dry-cleaner the other day he told me that many people who had seen it hanging there had said, 'If she doesn't pick it up, well, I'll happily have it.' So there we go. Maybe it really is perfect.

Perfect dresses are blissful when you find them. Their one-stop convenience, the not having to stress over what to match with what, the absolute certainty that they look good, is heavenly. Once you've experienced that, you are always looking for the next. They make all other dresses second-rate. But the only problem is you have to find them. And that means you have to shop for them.

Clothes shopping is one of the great divides. There are those who enjoy it so much that the activity of trawling through shops, trying on clothes, rifling through the rails, having conversations with sales assistants, is an end in itself. These are people who do not mind that they enter a cubicle with armloads of clothes and leave with them scattered all over the floor and nothing to take home. Or who don't have any problem with handing them back to the changing-room attendant saying that nothing had quite worked, while knowing that not only they but also the attendant would prefer that something had worked, not because they particularly care if you buy something, but because they don't want to have to deal with returning all the clothes to the shop floor. And then there are others, many of them, for whom the very thought of any of the above brings on a wash of sweaty anxiety. All that stuff to wade through. The ghastliness of choice. The physical act of being in a shop where you don't want to be.

Walking into a clothes shop or department store is a complex act. Why have you chosen there and not someplace else? Where do you start to look? Are you looking for something specific with a clear image in mind (guaranteed to fail), or are you browsing, not on Safari but through rails of actual clothes? Author Linda Grant writes a lot about shopping in her book of essays *The Thoughtful Dresser.* She says, and I'm sure she's right, that the first known use of the gerund 'shopping' is recorded in the *Oxford English Dictionary* as follows: 'Ladies are said to go a Shoping, when, in the Forenoon, sick of themselves, they order the coach, and driving from Shop to Shop.'

It's a wonderful citation. How often have I gone shopping when sick of myself? When the distraction of sifting through clothes with the inherent possibility of finding something – yes, ideally the perfect dress, but if not, anything that I think makes me look better – is an effective balm to the pressing difficulties of life or just that day. I have a memory of standing on a street corner in Paris outside Merci, a large concept store on boulevard

Beaumarchais, talking on my mobile to my friend and neighbour. Our sons were teenagers then and after that conversation I was momentarily able to distract myself from my unfounded fears about what might go wrong while I was away working, instead of being at home looking after him, by going into the shop and exploring the warehouse of homeware and clothes, and finding an expensive pale blue T shirt to add to my collection of expensive pale blue T shirts. For an hour or so it provided a welcome blurring of maternal preoccupations.

The reasons for shopping are so various. For Holly – a blonde woman with a Devon-cream complexion and a thing for red lipstick who I now work with from time to time – shopping provides a different solution. She always dresses in black and seemingly nearly identical black – long-sleeved tops and trousers. I asked her what motivates her to go shopping, curious that she buys the same things each time. 'Sadness is the reason I go shopping,' she tells me without hesitation. 'If something will make my life 2 per cent better it's worth the purchase, isn't it? Every time I have a new relationship I go and buy something because I think, "No wonder the one before didn't work, because I didn't have that jumper, or whatever, then."' The last time I saw Holly she had just bought a black leather biker jacket.

It's all of this, the escape, hope, anticipation, nirvana in the shape of that perfect dress, that is such a key part of shopping for clothes. Although online shopping may well provide those qualities, the experience is quite different. It's solitary, rather than an interaction with the sales assistants, a private transaction between you, your screen and your credit card. It is less sensual. You can't feel the fabrics or spot something out of the corner of your eye that just might be wonderful. You can't quite literally leave your environment and 'go' shopping, an activity which requires the participation of your whole body. The only movement required in shopping online is from your fingers. Online doesn't give me the same enjoyable hit as walking out of a shop with booty in hand, but it does give the same endorphin rush of possession. Until, that is, you try it on and discover that it doesn't fit. It's a million miles from fitting. The fabric is like a cheap dishcloth and the colour isn't even the same as it looked on screen. It's got a kind of yellow in it.

Although I own the perfect dress, there is naturally always room for more. Which is why I ended up scrolling away online yesterday when I should have been writing this. Within five minutes I'd swerved off-piste and instead of finding a new dress I had purchased a pricey Prada skirt that I had no previous intention of buying. I have no need of a new skirt. I didn't even want a new skirt. But there it popped up in a glorious rose print and I heard it calling my name. Never can resist a rose print.

I contemplated my future with the skirt. In the summer I could wear it with a pair of white sandals and a wafting white blouse, in the winter it will work with boots and a jacket. I imagine it will be the perfect (yup, there we go again) skirt for September, when I'll want something that hints of the summer just been but is substantial enough to take me places and to meet people where I need to look as if I am no longer on holiday.

When the skirt arrives I try it on. It fits perfectly, which is unfortunate since it now means I am more likely to keep it despite the fact it is not the dress I was looking for. I find David to ask whether he likes how it looks on me. Not because it would make much difference if he didn't, but even so it's always kind of nice to know. He says, 'That's a very nice dress. You'll like wearing that,' having looked at me for a few seconds. I leave the room, pointing out to him, 'It's a skirt!'

21.

T Shirts

It was one of those early spring days, just at the point where there's a new softness to the light that hints of warmth and overnight the blossom appears adding a delicious fuzziness to the previous months of stark, bare branches. Everyone was saying what a lovely day it was. It also happened to be the day before the day when we had first been meant to leave the EU – 29 March 2019. The unfathomable political chaos was making us all more than usually thankful for anything that was pleasant. Like that weather.

I sat in the hairdresser scrolling through T shirts on Net-a-Porter – 799 of them, on 14 pages – because that day it had become a matter of urgency for me to have a new T shirt. There was no specific reason for this, but I was convinced that a new T shirt was exactly what was needed to complete my life. I had in mind something with an emblem or a picture on it, and briefly toyed with a fabulously expensive Gucci number with Elton John's face circa 1975 and 'Someone Saved My Life Tonight' printed on it.

It wasn't that I don't already own more T shirts than anybody could possibly need. I particularly favour dingy, jailhouse colours – greys, taupe, khaki, stone – and there's one pale jade Gap crew neck that must be at least 25 years old that's still on fine form and travels with me on every holiday I take. But among them there wasn't one that hit the bull's-eye of what I had in mind. The T shirt that was going to suddenly make my whole wardrobe more interesting. Most of them are very much the lady-in-waiting-walking-two-steps-behind kind of things, rather than the stars of the show. The T shirt I had in mind that day, though, was going to be right out there centre stage, and, although obviously this wasn't going to happen, was going to make me look just a bit like Debbie Harry in her early Blondie days.

That's one of the wonderful things about clothes. They allow you to project the most unlikely visions onto yourself. They aren't hidebound by reality, which in the case of thinking about T shirts and myself might include any number of mutton alerts – back fat, bingo wings, sun damage, scraggy elbows. Instead, they allow you to indulge in escapism. Which is why I carried on in fixed pursuit of this T shirt with the determination of a pack of hounds charging after a scent.

There was a stage in the Nineties, post-grunge, when we were all besotted by layering T shirts. The designers of a Californian brand called C & C California came to London and visited the *Vogue* offices with huge bags of their T shirts and soon we were wearing their skinny thin-strap cotton vests under their longer-sleeved T shirts in what could become a very expensive mix. The fabric was very thin, which meant that really you had to wear more than one at a time otherwise your bra or breasts would show through. And they had a bit of a bias cut so that they clung a little to the body, while being extra-long so you could ruche them up flatteringly. It's one of the few times I remember T shirts being a fashion thing until right now, when slogan T shirts are everywhere.

In the 306 issues of British *Vogue* published during my time as Editor there was not one – not one – T shirt worn on the cover of the magazine. OK, pedants might spot a glimpse of a white one on March 1994's, under a bright pink Chanel jacket accompanied by the cover lines 'Dressing Up/Dressing Down' and 'Women Who Don't Want Children', although I can't swear that wasn't a vest. Or somebody could consider the blue-striped Jonathan Saunders crop top Beyoncé wore on May 2013's cover qualifies, but that was much more complicated than a simple T shirt. It's a curious fact, really quite intriguing, if you are interested in such things.

Certainly T shirts have a special relationship with fashion. There's an interdependency that, as in all such relationships, means that on occasion each party breaks away, determined to assert independence, before shortly after reuniting in ever-closer union.

T shirts don't really want to be fashion because the essence of them is that they should reject whimsical and capricious transience and glide endlessly on their own flight path. But their lasting popularity over the past 50 years is because they are not only utilitarian and classic, but are constantly being reinvigorated through fashion's transformative prism. Meaning? That T shirts need to have the imprimatur of fashion to exist outside of being simply a glorified piece of underwear. They need to keep being seen in a fashion context to hold on to their slot.

In this they are different to the plain white shirts, leather jackets, black turtlenecks and denim which I frequently published on the cover, all staples which on one level are not items of aspirational glamour either, but which all come loaded with a crate of style significance. Wearing them stamps you as a certain type of person. That is not the case with a T shirt, which is utterly neutral, which is also why it is the perfect message board.

When I last visited Kew Gardens it was a sunny October afternoon and I had just crossed the undulating John Pawson-designed bridge over the lake. Running towards me was a little girl in leggings and a pink T shirt bearing the words 'I am a feminist'. A year earlier Maria Grazia

The Christian Dior catwalk show in 2017

Chiuri, the then new and first female designer at Christian Dior, had sent the most famous models in the world down the Dior catwalk wearing T shirts with the message 'We Should All Be Feminists', paired somewhat incongruously with transparent navy tulle ballerina skirts.

Both those Dior T shirts and the little girl's, worn by very different sectors of the female population, owed their roots to one designed in 1975 by Labyris Books, the first women's bookshop in New York. On the front it spelled 'The Future is Female' and it featured in a photograph of a musician named Alix Dobkin, shot by her girlfriend Liza Cowan. Dobkin is wearing a somewhat shapeless white cotton number with blue lettering, over a long-sleeved blue cotton polo neck and a pair of brown cord trousers and the picture is captioned 'What the Well Dressed Dyke Will Wear'.

Fast forward to 2015 when two of a reissue of that shirt were snapped up by Annie Clark, a.k.a. the musician St. Vincent, for herself and her then girlfriend Cara Delevingne. The T shirt, a piece of clothing that started life as part of the American naval uniform at the end of the 19th century, has certainly, in the words of the Virginia Slims cigarette marketing slogan aimed at women in the Seventies, 'come a long way, baby'.

Full disclosure: I ended up buying that Elton John T shirt.

The original feminist T shirt, 1975

Michelle Obama at First Ladies Day in Rome, 2009

22

Sleeveless Shifts

On the morning of 2 April 2009 I was going to meet Michelle Obama. It wasn't only Michelle Obama I would be meeting but all 14 of the world's First Spouses (as they were termed), who were in London during the G20 summit hosted by the then Prime Minister Gordon Brown. His wife Sarah, charged with entertaining the spouses, had asked if *Vogue* would organize a commemorative group photograph while the menfolk gathered (as it happened, the attending spouses were then all women) to discuss the future of the world.

I spent a lot of time thinking about what I should wear for such a momentous occasion. Sarah had kindly asked me to join the group for lunch after the portrait, but I was also going to write about the day, and so was keen, as well as being seen as the *Vogue* Editor, to be the unobtrusive observer watching from the sidelines.

My journalistic heroine Joan Didion wrote in 'The White Album' (1968–78), her definitive essay about the Los Angeles of the Sixties, of the 'deliberate anonymity of costume; in a skirt, a leotard, *and stockings*, I could pass on either side of the culture'. I plumped for a dark grey cotton sleeveless shift with a green and yellow palm frond print that I had bought in a local boutique and a pale blue cardigan, thinking that might achieve the wallpaper effect Didion aimed for. The shift dress seemed to me to strike the right note – dignified but also relatively unremarkable.

Such dresses, with or without cardigan, have become a part of the First Lady kit, but that morning not a single First Spouse was wearing one. The role of First Lady is curiously opaque while simultaneously being highly visible. You are catapulted into the glare of the spotlight for no reason or clearly specified purpose other than your relationship to your partner. The guidelines for what you are meant to do are obscure, but the job description requires you to be diplomatic, cautious, discreet, charming and...well dressed. That is the thing everybody notices about you. What you wear. As a silent cipher standing alongside the main story, your appearance is not only the basis on which opinions are formed about you but, sometimes, the only way to say something when you are not supposed to speak.

In Britain the role is complicated by the fact we have royalty, unlike, say, the United States which has only one pre-eminent partner to gaze at. The royal family is privately wealthy as well as financed by the public purse, and Prince Charles contributes to the wardrobes of the Duchesses of Sussex, Cambridge and Cornwall, enabling them to dress the part. But political First Ladies are usually not privately wealthy and certainly not financed by the public purse.

While the British Prime Minster earns a reasonable salary, it's not enough to maintain a designer wardrobe for a wife (or partner) who might have been able to finance their own, were they not almost always required to compromise their own career and wage-earning capacity during their husband's term of office. So Sarah Brown was wearing a pleasant royal blue knitted two-piece from a mid-range label rather than anything pricey to host the spouses that morning, at the Royal Opera House, entertaining them with a dress rehearsal of the Royal Ballet's *Giselle* and a reading by J K Rowling (who wore the most fashionable item of the day – a pale pink Dior dress).

Vogue had only a few weeks to scramble the logistics, which for reasons of the intense security around the participants we code-named Betty. Most importantly we had to find a photographer who was available on the day and who had the star appeal necessary to handle a considerable number of women, all used to a degree of deference at home. Enter Mario Testino – in the event the only person who was flown in that morning on a private plane, having been in Hamburg the previous evening.

Each woman dressed to represent their nation as well as in their personal style. Gursharan Kaur, the wife of the

Indian President, wore an aquamarine and pale gold sari; Svetlana Medvedeva of Russia was in a trim, tweed lilac suit with a knee-length skirt; and Turkey's Emine Erdoğan was in the modest dress espoused by her husband's conservative Justice and Development party, pairing her long black abaya and white headdress with a pair of stonkingly high platform heels. Michelle Obama swept in last of all, in a swish of a wide green Jason Wu skirt and harlequin print blue Junya Watanabe cardigan. 'You can tell them I have a pink one too,' she told me, smiling with her impossibly white teeth and glorious fake lashes, as I asked what she was wearing for the piece I was writing.

Obama is one of the few First Ladies who has appeared utterly unafraid to embrace high fashion. Her pleasure in it was always wonderful to see. She unashamedly wore a broad range of designers, from Gap and J Crew to Versace, Azzedine Alaïa, Michael Kors and Moschino. And making the most of her well-toned arms she often wore the sleeveless shift dress, which was introduced to First Lady dressing by Jacqueline Kennedy.

The latter's wardrobe became a template for the whole nation's style during her White House years: neat suits, cropped jackets, pearls and fitted sheaths. In *Jackie Style*, the author Pamela Clarke Keogh claims that it was in the Fifties that Jackie had her first sleeveless shift run up, by her

Georgetown dressmaker Mini Rhea. She was being fitted for a new dress and while exploring the shape of the neckline decided that she wanted to show off her bare arms since she was proud of their shape. Rhea suggested that such a look was unsuitable for daytime, but Jackie ignored her and so 'one of the most influential looks of Camelot was invented in Mrs Rhea's little shop'.

When Meghan Markle appeared in her first TV interview about her engagement to Prince Harry, there she was, bare-armed in a green shift. Samantha Cameron, often noted as bringing an unusual fashion nous to Downing Street, was trim enough to frequently show off hers in a range of British designers. Successful female television presenters like Fiona Bruce and Emily Maitlis balance their on-screen gravitas with their ability to carry off a sleeveless shift without a trace of wobbling dimpled flesh about their upper arm.

Sleeveless shifts are signifiers of bicep power, for sure. Shapely upper arms are seen as demonstrations of confidence – and discipline. They denote application to the gym, age-defying rigour, a determination to triumph over the saggy pull of gravity. Were it not for Jacqueline Kennedy and her adoption of the simple sleeveless dress, perhaps we might never have reached this current thinking where a woman's achievement is, on some level, measured by how smooth the outline of her upper arms is.

23.

Handbags

These are the contents of yesterday's handbag:

- Red and yellow leather card holder containing Oyster card, two debit cards and three £20 notes
- iPhone
- Portable phone battery
- Very old pair of Apple headphones with a twisted lead
- Make-up bag with three lipsticks, eyeliner, tweezers, concealer
- Blue leather notebook
- 3 pens
- I packet of chewing gum
- Used ticket to the Lee Krasner exhibition at the Barbican
- 2 pound coins
- 2 black elastic hair bands
- Keys
- Paperback copy of *Chernobyl Prayer* by Svetlana Alexievich
- One left eye contact lens

The bag in question was a brown leather Prada tote. It must now be more than 20 years old, the leather softer than when new but otherwise unchanged. It's one of the 37 bags I own. There are among them a mini Louis Vuitton box shaped like one of their famous trunks; an unused green tweed Chanel mini bag; a floral linen Marni sack on leather straps; two suede leather Loewe numbers; a green leather Anya Hindmarch, with a message in my son's handwriting embossed in silver on the inside pocket from when he was about eight; a beautiful YSL brass clutch with a purple enamel iris-shaped clasp which no longer closes but which is far too lovely to give away.

Together, these bags are a legacy from editing *Vogue* during a period of time when handbags became the single most popular accessory, the cash cow that supported most of the most famous fashion brands in the world. A period of time when handbags were launched with the ludicrously inappropriate appellation of 'iconic', as if they represented anything more important than a money spinner for a fashion house. A period of time when the price of a handbag was raised hundreds of pounds to a more 'luxury' level simply because it could be. Because the elevated price alone gave it a currency. Not because of any intrinsic worth.

There was a different time when this was not remotely the case. Handbags are a relatively modern invention and it was not until the very late 19th century when the activity of carrying a bag began to be a sign of affluence rather than drudgery. Bags previously existed for men to carry various equipment while women's possessions were for centuries hidden below their skirts, hung on a chain or stuffed into small pouches, regarded as inconsequential stuff that needed no exposure. When the reticule, a small, usually fabric, pouch on a cord, appeared at the end of the 18th century it was the first time genteel women were seen carrying their belongings with them in public.

Bags can be viewed in the light of female emancipation, companions on the journey from the constricting confines of domesticity and domestic servitude. As increasing numbers of women began to be employed, travelling greater distances from home to the workplace became the norm. They required a bag to carry the day's necessities. But even those who didn't need to earn money were expanding the horizons of their daily existence, emerging from the drawing rooms and parlours of friends, to visit the department stores that were as exciting a development in the canon of shopping as e-commerce has been to our generation.

Department stores carried everything under one roof and most importantly showed it off. Previously stock would be hidden under a counter or in a back room, so that most purchases were of what you came in to buy. Now, these

mesmerizing emporia traded on the narcotic of display –
tempting you to buy things you didn't know you wanted.
Time could be spent just looking, and increasingly they
became destinations in themselves. Places where women
spent their leisure time – and money. They were thought to
be safe venues for women to socialize in outside the home
and, fascinatingly and crucially, provided loos, which
until then were impossible to find as you went about your
business in town.

By the 20th century, bags had a totemic value as a sign
of independence and stature. Women carried cash and
the more privileged had their own bank accounts and
the chequebooks that came with them. A few had keys to
their own property and some owned or had access to the
motorcar. Hence the rise in the Twenties of the expensive
and ornate clutch bag, an item intended to be noticed and
admired not just for itself but for what it might contain.

Lipstick, scent and powder compacts began to
accompany their owners for the first time, as applying
make-up in public became acceptable. Cigarette cases
and lighters were also carried, in an age where women had
begun to smoke. Obviously, bags had to expand to contain
these multiplying accessories to daily life.

The notion of a handbag as a statement of empowerment
seems old-fashioned. From an unrecognizably different

age. But maybe it's not so distant. In *Women in Clothes* –
Sheila Heti, Heidi Julavits and Leanne Shapton's fascinating
compendium on the subject – there is an anecdote from
writer Emily Gould about a pink 'purse', as the Americans
call their bags. In 2004, Gould writes, she was an assistant
in a publishing house and had bought a new handbag from
Marc by Marc Jacobs. 'Marc anything was the ultimate
status symbol for a specific kind of New York City woman,
the kind I aspired to be: someone with natural charisma,
a cool job, effortless and understated sexiness, and plenty
of cash.' The next day she takes the handbag to work and
hangs it up beside her desk where a senior colleague, P,
admires it, saying she wishes she could go out and buy one
for herself. 'What's stopping you?' Emily Gould asks. P
sighs. 'When you're married, when you have a child, you'll
understand,' the woman replies. Gould recalls, 'Back then
I had felt betrayed by P. If she couldn't buy a Marc by Marc
Jacobs purse, what was I working toward? She owed it to
me, to all assistants, to give us something to aspire to. She
owed it to us to dress for the job and the life we wanted.'

So yes, carrying a particular bag still signifies position,
achievement. In fact, more so than ever. Not any old bag
but a bag acknowledged by others to be desirable. In the
kingdom of handbags brand recognition is dominant.
Anybody can make a quilted leather bag on a brass chain

but they are not the Chanel 2.55. Ditto the famous Hermès Birkin. Anybody can buy a fake that looks like one of these. But they will know that it's a copy, they will feel that it's a copy. The cheap facsimile might look the same but it's an empty husk.

Since what an expensive and recognizable bag speaks of is the sum of far, far more than how it looks or what it contains, perhaps it's not surprising that the bag business – the It-bag – became so huge. Perhaps it's a logical progression for bags to become fashion rather than purely utility items. Things that can be yearned after and need to be continually updated, which is to an extent what fashion demands.

And for that change we can travel back to that leather Prada bag at the beginning. Not my actual bag but to Fratelli Prada, an established Milanese, traditional, family luggage business until the Eighties, when the daughter of the house Miuccia Prada became the chief designer. She transformed the brand by cleverly emphasizing the utility factor of a bag while at the same time making it an utterly desirable fashion piece. By producing a line of simple lightweight black nylon bags with the chic triangular enamelled Prada logo, she tapped into the desire for something more modern than the boxy big-name bags that had come before. Miuccia was well before her time in betting on this minimal style during the heady maximalist fashion age of the Eighties. But she was so right. Within five years Prada, now also with a growing range of women's clothing and shoes, became one of the most influential brands in the world.

Her success in launching a clothing business on the back of a bag prompted the bag rush that saw gem-encrusted Fendi Baguettes worth thousands of pounds being flaunted on the catwalk, vast showrooms filled with countless new Gucci styles every season and the increasingly important LVMH conglomerate hiring exciting designers to ramp up the fading brands they owned. Fashion was used as a *mise en scène* for the business of bags, which were so much easier to make money from. No sizing issues for a start. Anyone can gift a bag without worrying if it is going to fit. And nobody has ever said, 'Does my bag make me look fat?'

When Marc Jacobs arrived at luxury bag manufacturer Louis Vuitton he was encouraged to create fantastic fashion shows costing hundreds of thousands of pounds – all to further the sales of their growing bag collections. Shows which, in a supremely ironic statement, by 2007 featured Vuitton versions of the £2 plastic-coated checked bags sold in market stalls around the world – only these cost nearer a thousand pounds. Whereas previously bags had been accessories to clothes, the clothes were now accessorizing the bags.

At *Vogue* the pressure was on to feature all these new bags flooding into the market. By launching new bags every season, houses reduced the desirability of the previous ones and exposure in magazines was vital to ensure the success of the next love child. The only problem was that most of the fashion editors hated doing bag shoots.

For fashion editors, each shoot is like a miniature film with characters – the models – and story narratives. Even if what ends up on the page is a girl in a dress standing outside a restaurant followed by a girl in a trouser suit seated at a table inside, the fashion editor and photographer will have a more complex story going on in their heads. Think *Rear Window* rather than Boden catalogue. In the most remarkable fashion photography, the whole image is always more important, more memorable, than the pieces of clothing it shows.

So when it came to bags – well, not so easy. Combining the fashion editor's vision of the picture they wanted to produce with an image that pleased the big fashion houses who wanted their new bag to be shown clearly rather than stuffed under a table was always complicated.

Every season the regular accessory shoots would be one of my stress points. When a big house like a Gucci or Dior or Ralph Lauren, who spent millions of pounds supporting magazines like *Vogue* via their advertising, launched a new bag, they did not think it was enough to have it feature postage-stamp size in a line-up of 40 best bags for autumn. They wanted them each to be given star treatment.

The solution it seemed to me was to dedicate shoots entirely to accessories. Remove the landgrab of the models. Turn the objects into full page still lifes where they would be portrayed as objects of desire in a way they previously never were. Tellingly, the younger generation of fashion editors I worked with, who grew up in a world where bags had become such vital fashion items, had far more enthusiasm for putting them centre stage in their work than their older colleagues, for whom they were a distraction.

We may think little of buying a new bag even if we already own several, but even so the relationship between a woman and her handbag remains strangely personal. Our bags are visible to all, but inside there is our private world, housing our individual survival arsenal. For years I was claustrophobic, agoraphobic and prone to panic attacks. If you looked inside my handbag you would always find a bottle of water (not for thirst, but to sip should I get an attack), a Valium or later Xanax, and some kind of device for listening to the soothing tape a therapist had made. I always needed a bag large enough to carry these. Even now I will almost always have an iPhone and headphones to listen to music with if I feel fear moving in, and a book to distract me from that possibility.

Naturally, things being as they are, the counterbalance to this widespread bag ownership is that many of the very wealthy and famous increasingly carry no bags at all in public. The pendulum has come full circle. To appear bag-free is a contemporary indicator of success, indicating an aide hovering out of sight carrying the things you might need and allowing you an unencumbered appearance. Years back there were piles of that season's bags at the feet of fashion editors and celebrities on the front row. Now the ultimate in style is to go bagless. How often do you see a bag being carried on a red carpet?

One of the most poignant pictures of a bag that I have seen was not from a fashion magazine. I don't know what brand the bag is. I don't know who it belongs to. The photograph was taken on 19 December 2016 and the bright red bag sits upright on the floor of a photographic gallery in Ankara, at the edge of the frame. Behind is a white wall hung with a line of photographs and in front is the body of the Russian ambassador to Turkey, Andrei Karlov, who had just been assassinated by Mevlut Mert, who had posed as his bodyguard as Karlov gave a short speech, before pulling a gun from inside his jacket. In the picture Mert is still waving the gun.

The photographer Yavuz Alatan happened to be there that day in an unprofessional capacity, and most of the later attention given to the picture rightly focuses on the two men in their dark suits. One brutally murdered, the other himself shot dead 15 minutes later by the police. But it is also the bright red bag's story that I was surprised by. Who did it belong to? Why is it sitting there? How did it come to be witness to an assassination?

The assassination of Andrei Karlov, 2016

24.

Denim

A few years ago, I was telling a man I had once loved a story about arriving for lunch at Harry's Bar, a Mayfair members' club. I had forgotten that they didn't allow you to wear denim and I was wearing a denim jacket. Harry's Bar has the best chocolate mousse and bellinis in London and is the epitome of luxury, but they are non-negotiable on denim. So there was nothing for it but to remove my jacket and sit freezing and rather uncomfortable throughout lunch. He, rather than showing me any sympathy, replied that I shouldn't have been wearing the denim jacket in the first place and should have made more of an effort with what I was wearing if I was being taken to such a privileged spot.

I was hurt by this response for a number of reasons. First, I wanted him, as a measure of the fact that he knew me and understood me and had at one point loved me too, to think fondly of my arriving in a formal club in inappropriate clothing. Secondly, I wanted to think of him as the kind of person who would consider banning denim in this day and age faintly ridiculous. And thirdly, I wanted him to like the idea that I was wearing a denim jacket. He did none of these things.

I think now that I wanted him to like the idea of me in that jacket because somewhere I still feel that denim is invested with youth and sex. I wasn't thinking that when I told him the not very interesting story, but now, having thought at some length about the subject, I realize that is what was going on.

As I write, I am wearing a pair of blue denim jeans. I am not sure they suit me. When I tried them on in the store I had been unsure about them but was persuaded by the owner of the shop who was offering them to me as a gift, and a customer in the next changing room who agreed, that they suited me. They are wide-legged and high-waisted with a conspicuous zip fly and ring pull and frayed hems. They are the only pair I have of this shape, since usually I wear straight leg, slightly low-rise jeans. (Question: when did we start using the word 'rise' about the jean waistline?)

Even though I thought they made my relatively short legs appear, well...certainly no longer than they really are, it seemed churlish to keep dithering about whether to accept this pair and I also worried that I was stuck in a jeans time warp and should experiment with a different style. When I got home and tried them on again my initial opinion was confirmed. They looked horrible. No question. But having hidden them away for a year I have now put them on and they don't seem to look so bad. Maybe I have just got used to the new style that has since become hugely popular. Maybe they really don't look so bad. At any rate, that's why I'm wearing them today.

The team who designed them no doubt had an inspirational mood board in their office featuring a beautiful young woman in California – possibly on a San Franciscan street – in the early Seventies. It will be either in the faded Kodacolor of so many pictures of the time or more likely in black and white. She would have been dressed in a tiny T shirt and flared jeans, braless with a tanned face, long hair and white toothy smile. She will epitomize the desirable casualness of youth as well as looking fantastic in her jeans. It's entirely coincidental, but San Francisco is where blue jeans originated, in a store Levi Strauss opened to cater for the gold rush workers in the Sierra Nevada.

All a long time back from 1988 when Anna Wintour launched her first issue of American *Vogue*. She did so with a picture of a model wearing a Christian Lacroix Haute Couture jacket above a sliver of Guess jeans. The lead cover line was 'The real cost of looking good'. The photographer, Peter Lindbergh, shot this on an out-of-focus street and the model, Michaela Bercu, looked confident and relaxed with a big smile and loose tousled hair. The combination of denim and couture was interpreted as a deliberate statement of intent – the trailblazer of fashion moving into a high/low mix. As Wintour recollected years later, it was no such thing. The model couldn't fit into the skirt of the original Christian Lacroix suit and so they put her in jeans instead. That picture wasn't intended as the cover, but when Wintour saw it, as the savvy Editor she is, she immediately recognized that it looked compellingly fresh and different and would be a talking point for her first issue.

Now it seems utterly incredible that the idea of jeans on the cover of *Vogue* should be of any interest of any kind. In the intervening years this piece of clothing – which started life as the most basic utility wear – has morphed into its own luxury sector. 'Denim' is now a category like evening or swimwear. Whole floors of department stores are taken up with piles of it, brand after brand: skinny, regular fit, deep dyed, boyfriend, low waist, high waist, bootcut, narrow leg, etc. John Lewis, that Middle England bellwether, had over 50 styles at my last count.

It was a man called Warren Hirsh who came up with the idea that jeans could be a fashion item rather than an anti-fashion item. In 1976 he approached Gloria Vanderbilt, a member of one of America's most well-known wealthy families, to put her name to a line of expensive jeans, reckoning that there was a market for jeans that sounded elitist. She did and they sold. In their thousands. It was the start of a clothing sector in which there are growing numbers of brands that sell jeans for over £100, over £200, sometimes more. In the summer of 2019, Vetements, at that point the extremely fashionable line founded by the Georgian Gvasalia brothers, priced a pair of their distressed pale blue jeans at well over £1,000, which is a perfect example of fashion coming full circle.

Demna Gvasalia and his brother Guram's style identity was forged at a time when jeans could only be found on the black market in Soviet-ruled Georgia. Those who wore them were those who could afford to, often the children of people who were able to travel: privileged people such as diplomats or businessmen. It's no wonder that the brothers had a visceral understanding of selling denim at such a premium. During their childhood it was as aspirational as diamonds. But less easy to understand is why we, who have had access to a sea of denim for decades, sign up for wildly expensive jeans. How did denim accrue this patina of exclusivity and worth at the same time as being so strikingly commonplace?

Answer: through a combination of cool and sex. By the Fifties, denim had become a part of the growing teen culture. The massive post-war baby boom had created

Calvin Klein denim advertisement with Brooke Shields, 1980

an unusually large youthful population who wanted to separate themselves from what had been before. Jeans were a pillar of this look. For men. Inspired by movie stars like Brando and Dean, blue jeans had gathered a tough, bad boy cool, as clothes to break out of regulation life in. As Alexa Chung put it in a 2010 article for *Vogue*, 'James Dean wouldn't have smouldered nearly as well in chinos.'

But by the end of the Sixties, jeans had extended their influence to women. They had moved away entirely from connotations of physical labour and had become the uniform of the youth revolution. The noisy passion and rebellion and insistence of the youthquake of that time meant that it wasn't a huge step for jeans also to become sexy. The album cover of the Rolling Stones' *Sticky Fingers* featured an in-your-face pull-down fly. Much more recently Lana Del Rey sang, 'Blue jeans, white shirt, walked into the room you know you made my eyes burn' on her 2012 album *Born to Die*. And we understand her.

Calvin Klein, who once said 'Jeans are sex. The tighter they are, the better they sell', made headlines with an advertisement for his jeans modelled by the 15-year-old Brooke Shields, with the tag line 'Do you know what comes between me and my Calvins? Nothing.' At the time that line with its overt insinuation was thought controversial. But these were days when a respected director like Louis

Malle could make a film like *Pretty Baby* featuring the 12-year-old Brooke Shields working in a brothel. The ad, however, did Calvin Klein denim no end of good.

Genderless and sexy, democratic and elitist, ageless and yet invested with the chimera of youth, when you think about it the chameleon quality of jeans is nothing short of miraculous. And if that weren't enough, when I wear my favourite jeans, straight-legged with a bit of stretch – Roxanne by 7 For All Mankind, if anyone is interested – people often ask me, 'Have you lost weight?' What more could you want?

25.

Pink

I hadn't expected to buy a new lipstick. It was a steam iron I was after. But there I was on one of those grim August days when you are horribly aware of how summer has, without your realizing, almost trickled away.

The department store was busy with lunchtime shoppers and tourists in T shirts and shorts, and en route to the small electrical goods department I stopped off and tried out a bright, bubble-gum pink lipstick. To my surprise, in the artificial light of the store it looked quite good, and it made me feel that summer may not be reaching its end after all.

After buying the iron I went back to that make-up concession, making one of those calculations that go along the lines of: purchase of a dull, necessary household nature = purchase of something completely indulgent. But that particular shade was out of stock. Of course it was. In fact, the sales assistant said, she wasn't sure that it was even still being produced.

So things being how they are, as soon as I heard that it was going to be hard to find, it became a matter of vital importance that I get hold of it – Charlotte Tilbury's

Bosworth's Beauty was its name. Ten minutes earlier I had never heard of Bosworth's Beauty nor, as I've said, considered buying a new lipstick. But then, as I wove through the crowded street to another store, it was pretty much all I cared about.

It wasn't in the next store either. I tried to find an alternative, yet among all the many, many beauty brands nothing was exactly right. When I told the girl who was helping me at the YSL counter that the pink she suggested I try was too blue, she gave me a look, clearly confused by this statement. 'It's pink,' she said, winding it back up in the tube to show me. I replied yes, I knew it was pink but it was a blue pink. Some pinks are orange pinks, some yellow, some brown, some red. That elusive pink lipstick, when I eventually got my hands on it, was very definitely a pink pink. Pink's a colour with more lives than a cat.

Maybe that has something to do with why it is so attractive. Maybe that's why, in the process of writing this book, I have noticed how many times a piece of clothing I have a lasting attachment to is in some shade of pink. My first big teenage party dress and the Geography teacher's dress I wore when Sam was small are both in these pages. But there was also a baby pink Benetton cardigan I wore much of the time at home in my first flat. A piece of clothing which made me feel like the girl I really was, when I wasn't in the *Sunday Telegraph* offices trying to be an efficient newspaper editor. And the dark cyclamen pink Indian cotton dress I wore on my first date with Paul on a steamy hot night on Portobello Road. It's not as if my wardrobe is filled with the colour, but what is there has packed more of an emotional punch than any other, less flighty colour – brown, black, red, blue, green – of which there is much, much more.

It's hard to wear pink and be miserable. Whether that is because wearing pink does actually cheer you up – kicks in some serotonin – or whether one wears pink usually when one is already in an optimistic frame of mind, I don't know. If that were proven to be the case, surely we would sit in pink airline seats, receive pink tax demands and hang around in pink underground stations – all things that could do with a bit more of the feel-good factor.

However, a personal survey of everyday life has confirmed, to me at least, that when people see me wearing pink they are less likely to give me a hard time. I deploy it tactically. It's a useful colour to wear to tricky meetings of all kinds, from the conversation with your child's headmaster when he is threatening suspension to when you might be trying to persuade a small Arab Emirate to spend a ton of money on a magazine festival taking place on the other side of the world. Trust me, I know. Supremely superficial as this may be, wearing pink endows you with an often useful and entirely fictional softness that can help when the chips are down. It's an effective disguise and as stealthily lethal as a stiletto.

In a 2006 *New York Times* article titled 'What's Wrong With Cinderella?', the author Peggy Orenstein describes how, in 2000, a Disney executive made a decision to pick the Pantone colour 241CP – the sickly pink we are now all too familiar with – to unify the marketing of the female Disney characters. Cinderella, Sleeping Beauty, Belle and the gang were all packaged and often dressed in this pink and sold under a 'Princess' umbrella. The resulting commercial success is reflected in the mountains of pink packaging that is still regarded as catnip to a young female customer. There is, though, no conclusive evidence that the pink is a factor in the various objects' desirability because the target audience have an instinctive attachment to the colour or instead because they have come to associate it with things they enjoy.

Pink was not always attached to all things decorative and girly. Originally, babies of both sexes were swaddled and then dressed in unbleached natural fabrics which eventually began to be dyed pale blues and pinks. At first the pink was thought to be more suitable for boys. It was regarded as a more robust colour than the tranquil pale blue, and it was only in the 20th century that pink became so irrevocably associated with girls from birth onwards.

Pink may now be mired in the gender debate, but if you lift it out of that quagmire it is still a colour that radiates and catches the eye. The rose hues (rose being what pink was originally called) are traditionally associated with positive attributes: romance, tenderness, warmth and the natural beauty of sunsets, flowers and fruits.

I frequently used pink typography on the covers of *Vogue*. On one of his annual visits to London from New York, the then chairman of Condé Nast, S I Newhouse, told me that American *Vogue* undertook cover research every issue. I answered vaguely that this sounded like an interesting idea, to which he cuttingly replied, in his slow, hesitant manner of speech, which bore no resemblance to his razor-sharp brain, 'Aah...there...would be no... point...in...doing this just for...interest.' I got the message and, from then on, every month we sent a choice of covers and cover lines to a group of readers and potential readers. And almost always the cover with the pink type would get the most votes. Which didn't mean that we necessarily chose it. There had to be a limit to how many times we could rely on pink.

Pink suffers from being considered lightweight and insubstantial, but I have always found it a faithful friend.

I have a pale pink Marni coat that I bought in Milan about 20 years ago. It's knee length, in a wool and silk mix, with a slight Jackie O boxiness, large lustrous sandy peach buttons and a fur collar. Everybody who sees it loves it, even if they don't all love the fur. It's the kind of coat which suggests in the nicest possible way that you should put on a pair of large earrings and some delicate shoes and go out and have a good time. It's a coat that has never let me down. I'm looking at it now, hanging in front of me, confident and delicious. A companion in life, as all the best clothes should be.

26.

Bikinis

In 1968 I was wildly excited to be allowed to spend a holiday with my best friend Jane's family at their house in southern Italy. It was the first time that I had travelled abroad, other than as a very small child when my parents had taken me to a village near Saint-Tropez and my only memory was terror at seeing a grasshopper land on a table in front of me.

The journey was in those days long, and I was couriered from London by a fellow guest, Jane's older cousin, Grizelda. We flew to Rome and then took a nine-hour train journey south to the house, standing most of the time, with a suitcase of canned food Grizelda was taking out for her younger brother, who was also there and who was suffering from a bad case of measles.

The beautiful villa was built on a river with views of the nearby Tyrrhenian Sea, and I shared a large basement bedroom with six beds (known as The Pit) with Jane and her sisters Virginia and Eliza. We each had our own drawers for our clothes and I was amazed to discover that in their neat piles they had loads of swimwear, including numerous bikinis in bright colours and patterns.

Till then my swimming costume collection had consisted of a single black one-piece with a life-saving badge acknowledging me as competent in inflating a pair of pyjamas in the local swimming pool. Since I had never been on a holiday where much of the day was spent around a swimming pool or in the sea, it had never been necessary to have changes of costume. The notion that you might put on something to jump on and off lilos after breakfast, take it off to dry and then put on another piece of swimwear to wade down the river after lunch was entirely unfamiliar to me. Let alone to have a variety of new options for the days to follow. The two one-pieces I had with me, especially bought for the holiday, were serviceable but couldn't compare to the allure and variety of my friend's pool wardrobe. After a day or so I borrowed one of Jane's bikinis.

It's possible that early experience has had a lot to do with why I have always loved to wear bikinis. I still recall the thrill, even then at the age of ten, of seeing for the first time my tan line deepen every day where the top of the bikini pants met my skin. Of comparing the delicious contrast between my brown tummy and the bits of my body covered by the fabric. I would stand in the dim light of The Pit, its dimness exacerbated by the brightness of the sun outside, staring at myself in the mirror on the wall to admire my skin darken after a morning in the sun. It was also the first time I understood the idea of getting a suntan as aspirational, and given my natural olive skin lapped up the appreciative comments on the topic by the adults who were themselves soaked in exotically scented brown Ambre Solaire oil. The next year, when I was invited to stay again, I had my own bikini – a fluorescent pink and orange number – that highlighted how brown I could get.

It seems extraordinary that one woman, Coco Chanel, could be credited with making the suntan fashionable, but that appears to be the case. Dark haired and dark skinned, she tanned easily, and when she appeared after one holiday with a new, deep colour, this, combined with her impeccable sense of style, inspired other society women she knew to emulate the look.

Her tan was not the same as the ruddy, rough sunburned skin of a worker exposed to the elements. It was a new sign of affluence. Before the Twenties tanned skin was undesirable – similar to having calloused hands. Those considered ladies were shaded by clothes and parasols from the effect of the rays, and a lush, pale, creamy colouring was the standard measurement of beauty and privilege in many countries.

But with the arrival of new methods of transport – the motorboat, the car, the jet plane – attitudes were changing. These advances enabled briefer and increasingly desirable trips abroad, becoming the shape of holidays as we now know them. Bringing with them the suntan. Once the tan became fashionable it followed that so did exposing more and more skin – hence the bikini, which was an abbreviated version of the already established two-piece of the Forties, with its high-waist pants and cantilevered tops.

Bikinis are one of the great female divides. Some – many – women never consider wearing them. They hate the way they emphasize the stomach, bottom and breasts. They crave the more slimming structure of a one-piece that can compress, support and shape. They are uncomfortable with the bikini's degree of public semi-nudity. They don't want to expose the stretch marks of childbirth or the scar of a caesarean, nor simply the wobbly flesh of a tummy.

A few years ago I stayed at the Cipriani hotel in Venice for a conference. On the last day we had a free morning, and round the beautiful huge swimming pool, which leads straight out to the lagoon, were a clutch of elderly Italian women. They walked around the perimeter of the pool in bikinis, gilt-trimmed sunglasses and wedge-heeled mules, putting on huge floral swimming caps to take to the water, where they stood chatting in the shallow end. They appeared completely at ease with their bodies, even with the folds of skin concertinaed around their stomachs, and the swells of flesh around the straps. I plan, if I can, to join their ranks. Wearing a bikini at any age seems to me so vastly more pleasurable than feeling encased, like a sausage in a skin, and ending up with a great white whale middle, hidden from the sun and air.

But there is no denying that bikini wearing demands a deep dive of body confidence, especially the first outing of the year. At that point I always feel like the child who imagines that if they close their eyes and can't see, then no one can see them. If I don't look at my bumpy chicken skin, age spots, thickened torso and belly, no one else will spot them either. The one area that I can't ignore, though, is what happens around my bikini line.

Having thick dark hair I have battled with body hair all my life. I was the ten-year-old with hairy legs. This meant that as soon as I was old enough to get to a chemist with enough pocket money, I was engaged in the utterly unrewarding, expensive and Sisyphean task of its removal. First locked in the bathroom, spreading on vile-smelling Immac with the insufficiently minute spatula that came with the tub, which as anyone knows who has tried it almost always falls off all over the floor in great sloppy lumps and generally disappoints. Then, years later, costly and embarrassing waxing.

Body hair and I have a negotiated relationship. I lose some, keep the rest. I have always kept the dark hair on my arms, despite almost every beauty therapist suggesting I might like to get rid of it, and it lies pooled on the small of my back where I know I look like a baby bear. But on the 'if I can't see it, then it doesn't matter' principle, I leave it there. When it comes to the bikini line, though, I am not that nonchalant, and can't stop myself finding the odd straggle poking from the fabric as distasteful and disturbing as a fly in soup.

Which is in contrast to my general stance on pubic hair. This was determined as a teen watching the antics of those slightly older than me in the late Sixties and early Seventies, when pubic hair was something to flaunt not to get rid of. The sophisticated older girls of that time danced on the stage of *Hair*, romped naked at music festivals, their wide, dense bushes a symbol of liberation and sexuality. I can't say I love mine – not at all. The first time a man saw me naked I was sure he'd hate that hair, but he didn't and neither, it seemed, have any who followed. The thought of so many younger women who feel that they have to lose theirs almost entirely in order to be desirable, in order to feel clean, is sad. But, even so, come bikini time – off to Odette I head to have hot wax slathered around my upper thighs and ripped off while we talk about our children and where I am going to go on holiday.

The difference between the wearing of a two- and a one-piece is far greater than what is exposed by the different amount of fabric involved. Somehow, exposing our belly (not our abs, not our cleavage, not our lower back) seems to provoke extreme reactions. In 2017, shortly after I left *Vogue*, David and I were on holiday with friends in Greece. Our host was planning an afternoon on his boat and was trying to corral the large number of house guests down to the jetty where it was moored. In a rush I ran up to our bedroom to grab a towel and book. The room was painted in a mix of dusty blues and creams, the wooden balcony boasting one of the world's most beautiful views across the Saronic Gulf to the Peloponnese, and I felt a wave of pure contentment: to be there in this beautiful house, on holiday, heading off to swim in the calm, clear, turquoise sea. So before I left the room I took a snap on my phone of the reflection of myself in a small mirror and posted it on Instagram. I was wearing a blue, yellow and white Boden bikini.

We spent the afternoon bobbing around in a small bay only accessible by boat, snorkelling in the clear water, drinking cold wine and beers and dozing in the sun, returning to the house in the early evening. David went up to the bedroom to check his phone, returning to say he had had an email from a friend at the *Daily Mail*

Front page news in 2017 – I wore a bikini

who wrote that the picture of me in my bikini was 'news'. Slightly worried, and certainly curious, I checked my own email to find one from that paper asking if I would write a piece about wearing a bikini. I thanked them and said no. I couldn't imagine what I could say. What would the story possibly be? It wasn't like I had done something remotely interesting.

Wrong. Or so it appeared from the next day's *Mail*, which published a piece reporting that the sight of an unfiltered Instagram post (which they reproduced in a dauntingly large size) of a woman in her late 50s, who had just left the editorship of *Vogue*, wearing a bikini had collected thousands of supportive comments from other women. The day after, more papers and websites covered this unlikely 'story' while the *Mail* changed tack, publishing a piece by a female columnist saying I should have kept my 'wobbly bits' to myself and how I must be doing penance for having inflicted years of unrealistic body expectations on women during my years at *Vogue*.

Not for a second, not in my wildest imagination, had I thought I was making a deliberate statement about my age, leaving my job, my self-image. Nor had I considered it said anything at all about idealized images of beauty. I had thought I was putting up a candid snap of me looking happy, which would simply have been seen as such. I never dreamed the subject would hijack the soft news cycle for days. If I had intended to make any kind of point to the nation I might at least have done something about my hair and spruced up the background a bit. And possibly added a more forgiving filter which would have hidden some of the mosquito bites all over my tummy!

But I did none of these, and so happened Bikinigate.

27.

White Shoes

I said 'Lou, you gotta start new
And the first thing you gotta do
Is get some white shoes'

JACK TEMPCHIN, 'WHITE SHOES'

My first trip to the New York collections was in October 1992. I hadn't taken a long-distance flight in a decade because I was truly terrified of flying. Not a vague have-a-quick-vodka-at-the-airport apprehension, but the kind of fear that wakes you burning with terror for many nights before and seeps into your every thought for weeks ahead. I knew though that this trip was essential to introduce myself to the vitally important American designers, Ralph Lauren, Donna Karan, Calvin Klein, Tommy Hilfiger, who at that stage were some of the most generous advertisers in *Vogue*. Eventually the day came and I boarded the plane with a packet of Temazepam and my then boyfriend Paul, and prepared to die. In the unlikely event that I would survive I had booked a visit to the hairdresser for the morning I arrived.

New York is the city of the blow-dry, and I had been told that the man with the golden brush was John Barrett, an Irishman who had recently opened a salon in the Bergdorf Goodman department store. As I sat in his chair, with a view out over Central Park, he took my messy hair in his stride, assuring me that I would leave the salon in the more soigne mode he regarded as appropriate for a *Vogue* Editor. But, he said, I had to do something about my shoes. Didn't I know? Nobody wears white shoes after Labor Day (the first Monday in September).

That was one of the things I remember most clearly about the trip. There I was, in New York for the first time in 15 years, in one of the most exciting cities in the world, and his comment on my white shoes is what has stuck in my memory. What about the shows? The designers? Nope. Just that remark about my white shoes.

Flashback to *White Boots*, the Noel Streatfeild tale of the aspiring ice-skaters Harriet and Lalla, which was one of my childhood favourites, with a central character who it was possible to imagine I could actually be. For we were taught skating at our primary school. It was the only sport we learned. Every Thursday in the autumn and spring terms my class would travel to the ice rink on Queensway, just across from Kensington Gardens.

If we were lucky, we owned our own pair of glorious, white boots, but if we didn't then we would have to hire the far less alluring scuffed black ones that were pulled out from a cubby hole at the rink. We raced around the ice in a pack, but at regular intervals the rink would be cleared of casual skaters for a period of formal dancing. The music would change and we would pair with a friend to do the foxtrot or the waltz, which we had been taught. Looking back, the sight of a group of nine-year-old private school girls in cobalt blue uniforms foxtrotting on ice must have been bizarre. But we all loved our skating and were proud of our pristine white boots gleaming over our navy tights.

It was many years later that I bought my first pair of white shoes. They were in woven leather with low cone heels and were part of an outfit that included a pair of white cargo pants and a turquoise and white striped velour top by Katharine Hamnett. I had bought the whole ensemble to cheer myself up when I was fired as secretary to the A&R department of Arista Records, a job I had landed because I knew the man who was running the company.

It was my second job after leaving university, and the second job I had lost. One Friday afternoon, about four months after I had joined, I was called into my immediate boss Tarquin's office and handed an envelope containing a letter terminating my employment. He was very pleasant but gave me no reason for my dismissal, just saying I wasn't suited to the job and he was sure I would be happier somewhere else.

I always thought it had something to do with a one-night stand I had with the boyfriend of one of his closest friends. At any rate, the experience taught me three important lessons: 1) Don't sleep with the boyfriends of friends of your boss. 2) You might get a job through who you know, but that doesn't mean you will keep it. And 3), although at the time being fired is utterly miserable, it almost always leads you into doing something more interesting. If I hadn't lost that job, I might never have changed direction and begun my career in magazines.

White shoes tread the finest line between the right and wrong side of trashy. There is something delicious about their devil-may-care impracticality. There is nothing everyday about a pair of brilliant white shoes shining like diamonds on a city pavement. They hint of a pampered world without grime and stains. They are unashamed of their stand-out quality, especially in autumn when they carry an all-important insouciance about the wind, rain and dark nights ahead. But cross the tracks and they are completely the opposite. Then, scuffed and grubby, they are a stalwart of the goose-pimpled Saturday night booze

Wearing my Manolos at the Business of Fashion 500 gala, 2016

fest in freezing winter cities. They have the extraordinary ability to signify both poverty and privilege.

When I see a pair of white shoes they call to me as no others do. I imagine them worn with denim, with black tights or tanned bare feet, glimmering at a party. Loafers and courts, sandals and pumps, ankle boots and trainers. Over the years I have bought them all. Each new pair brings a sparkling sense of opportunity. They add a spritz of energy to the most ordinary clothes.

During my last five or six years of *Vogue* I was rarely photographed in anything other than a pair of 90mm Manolo Blahnik white courts. His more usual heel heights were either lower at 75mm or higher at over 100mm, but 90mm was perfect for me. I could walk easily and even run in them if I needed, but they gave me the extra height I have always craved. They were never, ever, not for an instant, uncomfortable.

They weren't part of his permanent collection and I was lucky enough to have Manolo make them for me. Every year they would arrive in the office nestled in their soft chamois shoe bags, lying in white shoe boxes, utterly immaculate. There was and still is something about their lightness, brightness and of course whiteness that made me happy.

Magazine leaving cards traditionally feature a picture of the leaver on the front cover of the magazine. When I left *Vogue*, mine – a head shot taken by Mario Testino several years earlier – included the cover line '101 Ways to Wear a White Shoe (Bespoke Manolo preferred)'.

My leaving card from Vogue, *2017*

28.

The Big Ticket Dress

In Rosamond Lehmann's 1932 novel, *Invitation to the Waltz*, there is a description of dressing for a big ticket event, in this case 17-year-old Olivia Curtis's first dance. Urged on by Olivia's older sister Kate (against her mother's natural preference for 'more delicate shades'), her parents have bought her a bolt of flame-coloured silk as a birthday present. Her mother tells her to get it made up as a dress for the dance by the local dressmaker, Miss Robinson, 'in some very simple way', but Miss Robinson is having none of it and decrees she will make Olivia 'look posh', dismissing her mother's instinct for discretion with the damning observation, 'Your mother's not one for what I call show, is she?'

Come the night of the dance, the weeks of thrilling anticipation and nerves come to a head as Olivia is getting dressed, her gown having only just arrived. Lying on the bed before her, it is 'smooth, inviting, brilliant'. As she slips the dress over her head she can immediately tell that it is, predictably, a disaster. The 'clumsy lumpish pointless draping' encapsulates all that she fears her presence at the dance might be and she threatens to rip it off and burn it and not go to the dance at all. Until her sister points out that she has put it on the wrong way round and she re-emerges 'delivered from despair, once more a young girl dressed for her first dance – not a caricature of one – able again to compete with and appreciate others...'

Oh yes. How much of that description does one recognize when it comes to weddings, bar mitzvahs, proms, anniversary bashes – all of those big ticket occasions which require you seriously to dress up. Literally. Dress in a way that rises above the ordinary. That raises the bar. That lifts you out of the everyness of everyday. Truly dress up, in an intoxicating mixture of fear, anticipation, expectation and hope.

My first such event was a party held in a beautiful ballroom, one of the few remaining, of a private house in Chelsea, given by two boys who were the sons of friends of my parents. They were 18 and 16, and I was 13 and utterly terrified. Up until then parties had only involved a group of girls from my class at school going to the cinema for a film and then maybe to somewhere to have a hamburger. This party was obviously something of a quite different order.

The dress I found for the evening was from Forbidden Fruit, a shop on a corner of the King's Road with piles of mirrored dresses and waistcoats and shawls from Afghanistan and India. It was midi length in a very pale pink silky material with a grey forget-me-not print, long sleeves and a neckline that laced up. When I showed it off at home, to my complete chagrin my mother insisted that a modest piece of fabric was inserted between the laces and my skin, removing the one element of daring in this softly romantic dress.

The party was filled with public schoolboys from Eton and Harrow in black tie, with their white shirts and teeth glowing in the ultraviolet lighting that also dramatically improved everyone's dodgy complexions. The air was thick with Eau Sauvage aftershave. That winter's hit, 'Lady Barbara' by Peter Noone and Herman's Hermits, played again and again, a rather soppy song which, with the benefit of hindsight, had absolutely nothing to recommend it. But I danced with a cabinet minister's son who held me clammily against him and somebody who I didn't know kissed me during a slow dance. My father picked me up at midnight and my world had changed. Ahead of me was a lifetime of parties where I might meet somebody who might kiss me during a slow dance. And I was wearing a pink dress which I never wore again. There was never another occasion that could live up to the memory of that one.

So often we never wear the dress again that we have worn for such precious occasions. The dress is a part of something unique, often a once-in-a-lifetime moment, and wearing it for a lesser event would ruin it, evaporate the

It's Fashion! gala with Prince Charles and Tom Ford, 2001

heady sense of import that is deeply embedded in its every fold, button and stitch. So those dresses become costumes that hang there unworn, our own museum pieces.

My mother was and still is fond of quoting Nanny in Nancy Mitford's *The Blessing*, who tells the central character, Grace, as she is getting dressed on her wedding day, 'Never mind, dear. Nobody's going to look at you.' It's sort of a family joke that our mother might say whenever she or I or my sister were getting dressed up for a big occasion, although it would also be employed self-mockingly whenever we might be getting in a state about what to wear, when, really, it kind of didn't matter. Although it always does kind of matter – and that was the joke.

There were three occasions during my time at *Vogue* when I acknowledged that it really did matter what I was wearing. In all of them I was the host and couldn't pretend, which was quite often my defensive default position, that there would be so many other people there that my own outfit would simply be background music. The first was It's Fashion! in 2001, a fundraising gala held at Waddesdon Manor, the Rothschilds' 19th-century French-style chateau in Buckinghamshire. The cohosts on the invitation were myself, Madonna (who on the night had to be substituted with Kylie Minogue) and Lord Rothschild. Guest of honour was Prince Charles (who seemed delighted with

Kylie on his right-hand side), patron of the recipient charity, Macmillan Cancer Relief.

I had come up with the idea that we could turn the enormous lawn into a contemporary Field of the Cloth of Gold, inviting designers to pitch their own pavilions, in the way that knights would have during the long weeks of the famous summit-cum-tournament between Henry VIII and the French king Francis I. And to my relief and great excitement, many of them agreed to do so.

Versace, Armani, Gucci, Burberry, Chanel and others each brought a tent-sized portion of their world to a corner of Buckinghamshire. Donatella Versace's pavilion had its own DJ, Burberry's was plastered in their new black and white advertising campaign and Tom Ford, who had bravely been the first designer to commit to the scheme and was hosting the Gucci pavilion, had insisted it be in black cloth (in an otherwise sea of white). In his miniature Gucci world he had installed a floor of scarlet rose petals and a full-frontal hologram of a model, naked bar a pair of high-heeled Gucci shoes. It was an extraordinary evening, but even in the company of such a gathering the 'nobody is going to be looking at you' rule really couldn't apply to what I was to wear as host.

I thought I should wear a British designer, but one that wouldn't cause offence to anyone else, i.e., one that was not in direct competition with Burberry or indeed the other companies that had spent a lot of money to pitch their tents – paying to take dinner tables, flying in their guests. So I plumped, in an admittedly slightly eccentric way, for the house of Hardy Amies, who could make me something bespoke. Hardy Amies as a fashion name had zero credibility by this time, but I still have that dress and it still fits beautifully; floor length, sleeveless black, with a black lace, boat-shaped neckline that tapered into the narrowest of straps on my shoulders. I brightened up the dress by draping a heavy pale turquoise satin shawl around my arms in the expectation of a classic chilly June night and my shoes were made by GINA in a sample of the same pale fabric. I borrowed incredible diamond earrings from the Bond Street jewellers S J Phillips and a huge aquamarine ring, the colour of the shawl, from the West End jewellers Bentley & Skinner. After the party the earrings had to go straight back, Cinderella-style, but I bought myself the ring as a congratulations gift for the evening. A few years later I lost it, most likely when I took it off to do the washing up after a dinner at home one night. The thing about losing jewellery is that you never know where you lose it, do you? And it's never the Topshop ring that disappears.

I would say that altogether I looked elegant and hostess-like as I escorted Prince Charles into the pavilions, my heels piercing the grass with each step. I felt as if I was wearing the correct costume to see me through. It wasn't a joyful dress, though – more a piece of highly refined equipment.

The second occasion was 18 September 2007, when I cohosted a gala opening dinner at the V&A for the exhibition 'The Golden Age of Couture'. This was sponsored by Dior, whose artistic director at that time was John Galliano. John still had his eponymous label, which I thought would suit me better than Dior, so I asked, nervously, if the Galliano team would be able to make me a dress for the evening.

Although this was three years before John's career imploded with his crazed anti-Semitic rant in a Parisian café, even then he was not in a healthy place. From the beginning his 'people' – the tribe that all designers have in place to protect them from having to engage in dull detail and sometimes difficult conversations – had made it clear he might not be able to attend the opening. His 'people' were his protectors but also in a way his jailors. The extravagant lifestyle funded by his employers helped him to hide from the inconveniences of the real world while keeping him fixed on the treadmill of the ever-growing number of collections. They were hoping to keep their golden goose alive, but unintentionally they were enabling him to self-destruct.

So I wasn't remotely surprised when I travelled to Paris for my first fitting that it was members of his design team and not the man himself that I met as I turned up at the Galliano headquarters. There I was measured for a toile, and looked at swatches of fabrics and explained the bits of my body that I wanted to disguise – tummy and thighs – and the bits I didn't mind displaying – breast, arms, ankles. To be honest I was relieved not to have to expose my body to Galliano's personal scrutiny. I didn't know him and I was afraid of what he might think of it.

The process of being fitted for a dress is curiously intimate and intrusive. You cannot hide from the gaze or the tape measure. You hope that this creation will be something that takes you as the raw material and transforms you into an object of perfection. And you know all the while that this is highly unlikely. But it is for that possibility that people are prepared to pay thousands of pounds.

Full-length dresses have always bothered me. Perhaps it is because I am not tall enough to carry them off, but there is something about their drama that demands something from me that I don't possess. So we agreed that the dress would be calf-length, in a delicious deep raspberry chiffon with a boned bodice, Galliano's trademark bias-cut skirt and a fuchsia silk, matador-style bolero.

It was, and still is, beautiful. But, like that much earlier party dress, it has remained unworn since that evening when I stood just inside the entrance hall of the Victoria and Albert Museum greeting the guests, a rollcall of who was a certain kind of who that year. The model Natalia Vodianova unbelievably appeared only three days after giving birth, looking stunning in an oyster silk Givenchy mini dress and vertiginous heels. Nigella Lawson was magnificent in a long navy velvet gown. Kate Moss and Courtney Love were twinned in cream Givenchy silk (Kate trashed hers on the steps of the museum as she left the party). And the rock star Prince, who was performing in London, arrived as an exciting last-minute guest with an enormous entourage.

It was a night of deliciously glamorous ostentation, raising funds for the world's largest museum of decorative and textile arts. It took place almost a year to the day before the Lehman Brothers crash, when the banking system came tumbling down.

And my last big ticket dress was a sequined shift the designer Erdem Moralioglu made me to wear for the 2016 *Vogue* Centenary gala dinner. The original was on his catwalk in the spring, an undulating gunmetal grey, long-sleeved, high-necked dress that glimmered like Victorian silver, traced with a pattern of black embroidery. Erdem and I took the ingredients and mushed them around to make the dress I wanted, starting with a scrap of fabric and his deft sketch that showed it on a woman with a small head and boyish crop, long earrings and a slender body. Like all couture dresses, rather than appearing fully formed it grew over three months, changing colours, lengths, shapes each time we met in the sea-blue changing room of his Mayfair store.

Erdem suggests a train, and I say no. He wonders if perhaps we can make a theatrical cape to pair with it: again I disappoint. And he is aching for the drama of long. But I am adamant that I want short.

When the dress arrives, a few nights before the party, in its white cotton garment bag with the chic black lettering of ERDEM, I rush into the loos at the office to slip into it. If something looked good in the ugly lighting of the *Vogue* loos then I knew it would look good anywhere on earth. So as I stare at myself in the mirrored wall opposite the basins I am hugely relieved, knowing that if nothing else goes well that night, my dress will stand the ultimate big ticket test. It is a dress for a person at the centre and not an outlier. When I wear it, it will be in the full knowledge that this will be an occasion when what I wear should, and does, really matter. And that, yes, somebody, quite probably everybody, will most definitely be looking at me.

Model Adwoa Aboah wearing trainers in Paris, 2018

29.

The Trainer

It is icy on the pavements. As my bus travels down Park Lane towards Hyde Park Corner, I hear a woman in the seat behind me discussing a fall her companion has taken. It's not quite clear where or when this took place but the man she is discussing it with has a brisk put-up-and-shut-up attitude, whereas she sounds uncertain. 'I'm always terrified of everything. Which is a terrible disadvantage,' I hear her say.

I wonder what she looks like, the owner of this voice, full of a particular type of middle-class Englishwoman's attitude – that of self-doubt and denigration. Soft curly grey hair, pale skin, dim blue eyes, I imagine. 'Oh dear,' she continues with a deep sigh, 'can't change now.'

As my stop approaches I stand up and take the opportunity to look at them – and they are just as I imagined. He in a stiff tweed jacket, his grey hair thinning and neat and she buttoned into a nondescript blue coat, with a face that would have once been pretty, but is now unremarkable. She is gesturing to my feet and I can vaguely hear her pointing out the fact that my shoes are practical on an icy day like this. 'Sensible,' she is saying. Following her gestures, he glances at my feet, registering nothing. He sees, I suppose to his mind, a pair of ugly but possibly quite practical sports shoes on a woman who is also wearing a rather fancy coat with a shaggy fake fur trim. I would guess he finds the whole thing a rather odd look. But then again he probably doesn't have an opinion on this.

What I am absolutely sure of is that neither of them had any idea of the cost of the white rubber-soled trainers that I was wearing. They were a pair of £400 Balenciaga Race Runners, bought in Athens during a sudden downpour when the nearest immediate shelter was the Balenciaga store on that city's equivalent of Bond Street. I very much doubt that couple on the bus could have imagined such a pair of shoes could cost that kind of money or that anyone could conceivably think it worth paying such a sum for them.

But I did just that. They were in the window of the shop where David and I dashed for shelter. With a gently tapered white mesh toe, and a black grosgrain band cutting across the smooth, matt white leather, they were the most elegant trainers I had ever seen. They were the last pair and just happened to be in my size. Of course, I had to have them, even though I had never considered myself the kind of person that would drop that kind of money on that kind of shoe. After all, I wasn't some kid with a trainer-brand dependency.

There is an irony in the fact that trainers, now considered a democratic piece of footwear, evolved, like their name suggests, from sporting footwear like plimsolls and then sneakers. Sports of any kind and the equipment that goes with them were originally a luxury of the leisured adult. Most people had their hands full keeping themselves housed and fed with no extra time for the convivial playing of sports.

So the notion of trainers as egalitarian, as a style rooted in the street, is entirely contemporary. By the Eighties, companies like Nike, Adidas and Puma realized that they could sell microbranded pieces for a premium – like the Air Jordan and Adidas Stan Smith. Their widespread adoption by the rap and hip hop communities gave them the initial lift-off needed to become aspirationally fashionable, but early on it was by no means a slam dunk that trainers would become the expensive fashion items of today, as well as the most popular type of footwear across the globe.

It would have been inconceivable to my eight-year-old self, as I laced up my pair of canvas plimsolls in preparation for my weekly tennis lesson, to imagine that these shoes could be regarded as anything other than something you wore for games. Games, note. Not sport. Small change, big difference, as we liked to write in fashion captions at *Vogue* when we talked about a new heel shape or a different way to roll up a cuff.

Plimsolls are soft and gentle. In the Nineties, dyed dusty pastel shades of pink and turquoise, they had a moment in the sun as a yum-mum thing – worn with printed dresses that harked back to the tea dresses of yesteryear, or maybe a pair of shorts and a T shirt to take the children crabbing. But my childhood white ones, kept clean with a weekly sponging from a tube of Kiwi polish that always got stuck on my hands, were very definitely only worn for games.

However, trainers and their direct antecedents sneakers, like Keds and Converse, belong to Sport. Capital S. They are competitive and androgynous, ready for action and now an intrinsic part of the world we live in today, where the notion that we all exercise, that we all want to keep fit, has become so accepted that the clothes you might wear to achieve this have become as ubiquitous as a suit.

I clearly remember a conversation in my 20s, when I was told by a woman only a few years older than me that once you hit 30 you had to exercise. We were in a wine bar, halfway through a bottle of white Chardonnay, with our packets of Marlboro on the table. I felt slightly sorry for her – for having reached an age where she was worrying about her body being in decline. It was one thing not to feel particularly delighted by one's shape, but to envisage it in active decline was something else.

At that point I didn't know anybody who exercised. The idea of running, lifting weights, treadmills, lunges, planks – that worldwide vocabulary – was as unused as Esperanto. The idea of deliberately getting fit, or maintaining your fitness, was not only something that in my teens and 20s was utterly irrelevant, it was also, like playing bridge, something that you might consider taking up when you got old and wanted something to fill your time.

Sure, we might have heard of Jane Fonda and her aerobic burn, and in London of a woman called Lotte Berk, a sparrow in a black leotard whose classes were for wealthy women in Chelsea. And some people around this point began to attend the Pineapple dance centre in Covent Garden – kitted out in colourful tights and even more colourful leg warmers. But the notion of regular exercise was pretty rarefied. Anyway, most of the older women I knew, parents of friends, work colleagues, looked perfectly good without forcing themselves on to a 5K run three times a week. And they seemed relatively healthy. A thought that often comes to mind when I am trying to get myself to do that very 5K now.

But only a few years later, in the Eighties, along with chains like Pret a Manger or Starbucks and mobile phones, gyms arrived in the UK. And then personal trainers, marathons, yoga centres and Pilates classes. Fitness was sold as the new panacea for the masses. Instead of exercise being a way those heading relentlessly towards middle age might feel they were gaining some control of that unavoidable process, it was also for young people eager to get the hottest bods possible. Guys perfecting their six-packs, girls aiming for a washboard tum. At some point lunch hours, previously a time when you might sit in a park with a sandwich and a book, or moan about the bitch who was your immediate senior in the office over a glass of cheap red and a spaghetti carbonara, became a work-out opportunity. And now, more than 30 years on, wander any city centre in the early evening, early morning or lunchtime and look up one or two storeys above the street and you will see us there, a gym army in training, on cycles and treadmills, tuned into a Peloton programme or sweating it out on the StairMaster. Burning calories as if our lives depended on it. Which, of course, we are frequently told is the case.

And trainers? They are worn by every person in those gyms or pounding round parks and streets. But instead of being relegated as part of a sports kit to that area of our lives, trainer creep has infiltrated every aspect of social interaction. The kid doing wheelies just outside the council estate is wearing apparently the same (though not actually the same) shoes as the Silicon Valley honcho working on a disruptive app. From under the abaya of a wealthy Emirati woman in the Dubai mall will peep the same red and green Gucci stripes as the Portuguese office cleaner who bought hers from a street market. The Wiltshire grandmother who likes to keep busy lives in hers because nothing else matches them for comfort, as does her granddaughter who was probably bought a trainer as her first pair of shoes and views them as a fashion item, in constant need of upgrade.

It won't last, it can't. That's the thing about trends – and the mass popularity of trainers is a trend – they emerge from the lives we are living and vanish similarly. Now that we can sit at a kitchen table and shout commands to a speaker to get things done, rather than actually move and do it ourselves, will the trainer continue its rule as the footwear of mass choice? As we move towards an existence where we start to do less not more, where VR and AI allow us to be places that our bodies aren't and to have our functions replaced by technology, what place will the keep-us-on-the-move trainers have? And, on a more basic level, now that everybody you see on the Tube, on the buses, in the supermarkets, in the park, is wearing them, is it possible for the trainer to remain this astonishing, communally recognized object of desire?

On a Sifnos beach, August 1978

30.

Holiday Wardrobes

Britain is baking in the tropical temperatures of the African plume the day Boris Johnson becomes British Prime Minister. The heat is of a quite different order to that usually experienced in the city. The metal lampposts burn. People are crossing the road for shade. Cats lie sprawled, motionless. It is more Lagos than London.

I am wearing a pair of trousers in a dusty pink, pale cotton, which were run up by my yoga teacher, Audrey. They are beyond loose, really just a couple of rectangles tied around the hip in a superfine, almost transparent fabric. As I walk to the local shops I catch sight of myself reflected in a car window, my stomach hugely protruding in a mixture of water retention from the heat and the tie bunched around my abdomen. Nobody, not even my most devoted admirers, could say I looked anything other than fat, but that doesn't matter. These are my happy pants. When I wear them it is always hot and heat is what I love. The way that it slows everything down, the balmy early morning and steamy, body-temperature evenings.

Holiday clothes are about escaping from the daily world, and, on that day, wearing a pair of trousers that I usually only wear on holiday was an antidote to my very real concern about the implications for the country of what had just happened. A line from the Louis MacNeice poem 'Snow' spun in my head: 'World is crazier and more of it than we think'. The trousers were my response. I deliberately wore them not only to keep cool but to create a personal carapace of casualness when it looked to me as if the world had suddenly become several degrees more unpredictable. A hazy pink cotton pair of trousers can help in that way.

One drawer of the chest of drawers in our bedroom is where I keep most of my holiday clothes. Much of it was bought travelling. The translucent cotton smocks from a boutique found down a side road on the island of Hydra, the thin blue and white shirtdress from a shop on the main street of Deià in Majorca, a sleeveless pale green and black block-printed shift from a huge vintage store on LA's Melrose Avenue. The drawer is completely crammed with years of such accumulation – another piece added after each trip, souvenirs of the different places.

When I see them piled on the floor waiting to be packed I am immediately transported from the usual world where the cat needs to be fed, the bed made, the vacuum bags replaced, the roses deadheaded. Where my to-do list is forever only half completed and I am concerned about the work I am behind with or, worse, that I may run out of work to do. To a place where no such considerations have a place, and nor do they on the clothes that I take to wear there. The only problem in front of me at this stage is what to pack. They can't all travel with me each time but I have an attachment to this sartorial family and feel sorry for them if they get left behind. I hate to think of them stuck in an airless drawer, waiting for another opportunity to get out.

The oldest item in the collection is a pale stone cotton skirt from a Martin Margiela diffusion line, with a drawstring at the waist, that I bought in Paris when I was whiling away an hour between fashion shows years back. It has been worn to countless European supermarkets to stock up on the local wines and cheese and mosquito repellent, and has accompanied me on endless car journeys trying to find my way around a new neighbourhood, in times before we all were able to rely on a satnav and had to keep pulling in to check the map, wondering which way up we should be looking at it. The skirt reaches the knee and the cotton, even after decades, still makes a nice stiff shape when it's newly washed. I put my trust in that skirt like the reliable housekeeper on the holiday. It's a relief to know it won't let me down.

The second oldest is a green and white print silk slip dress. It didn't start our life together as a holiday dress.

I bought it in a small shop that sold pottery and a small selection of clothes in a Notting Hill mews and I ended up wearing it at the party I gave in my garden to celebrate the day I received an OBE in 2006. But now all these years later it has become a holiday staple, primarily because I am too thick around the waist for the bias cut fabric to be remotely flattering, which is something I care less about on holiday.

For me holidays have always been an opportunity to relax in terms of appearance, but that's certainly not the case for everyone. Holidays can be the complete opposite. They are an opportunity to dress up, to wear things you don't usually wear and to buy exotic new bits and pieces that have no place in your usual existence. An opportunity to wander around those sections that spring up in stores around April to tempt us with thoughts of our summer holidays, filled with turquoise and white fabrics and the ubiquitous gold trims and tassels, as if there is a large constituency of people who are tempted to channel their inner belly dancer during a fortnight in Majorca.

And why not? Isn't that the point? Holidays are where we feel more free to choose what we want to be. For every person like me who would never consider blow-drying their hair on holiday and is happiest in the evening in a pair of saggy blue cotton trousers (also decades old) and a smock top, there are those who love to indulge in massaging oils and serums into their sunbaked skin and experiment with make-up and new clothes.

When I was younger I felt different. Holidays then were often an opportunity, if not for love, then for what could pass for romance. Of course I cared what I wore. I wasn't exactly in *Love Island* body-con dresses, minuscule bikinis and high heels, but I packed clothes that I hoped made me look a bit sexy – I certainly wouldn't have contemplated the kind of things I wear now.

This is not because I have no desire to appear sexually attractive. Nor that I crossed a Rubicon when what I wear became irrelevant to how sexually appealing I might be. But the relationship between how I dress and how I imagine I am sexually perceived is different now. As I assume it is for most people. I have a permanent partner – I'm not trying to attract a new lover. I don't need somebody else to fancy me – though I would be lying if I pretended that I wouldn't like that. I have a grown-up son whose friends are around and I can enjoy how wonderful they look with no need to compete. I have a body that shows all the wear and tear of age.

When once my holiday wardrobe would have exposed as much naked flesh as it could, I would never now wear a skimpy T shirt dress or a scarf tied around my breasts as a top or a pair of tiny shorts (correction, I never wore a pair of tiny shorts). Not because I feel it is inappropriate but because I would look terrible. And that is the calculation that we all have to make when it comes to our age and how sexually explicit our clothes are. That calculation is different for everybody. Our circumstances, our history, our profession, our relationship with our bodies, are all factors. There is no absolute measurement of right or wrong.

It's a different life stage from when, at the end of my first year of university, I met a man at a party who asked me out to dinner the next night (in 1978, that's what men did). He was 30, 10 years older than me, and when I went home with him after that dinner he suggested I join him on the holiday he was taking a few weeks away. I accepted. As I did so I knew it was pretty random. We hardly knew each other and this was not the kind of thing I did. Neither have sex with someone on the first date, nor agree to go on holiday with them. I was and still am a pretty cautious type. But I thought it was time to become more adventurous, and this was the kind of thing I thought a more adventurous person would do.

A friend of his had written a blockbuster thriller and was spending part of the proceeds renting a house on the Greek island of Sifnos for himself and a group of his friends. My boyfriend, if we can call him that (and he certainly didn't), travelled there in advance of me since I was finishing a holiday job. I scoured the classified ads in the back of the *Evening Standard* for a cheap charter flight and found a late-night return to Athens for £90, which was then, in the days before budget air travel, a cheap flight. I arrived alone at the airport and waited till dawn to take the eight-hour ferry ride from the port of Piraeus to the island.

From the outset the house party was an exercise in dysfunction. One girl was a diagnosed manic-depressive, adorable and kind but completely stoned much of the time on a cocktail of barbiturates, and often only appearing by late afternoon. The host's girlfriend, who was skin and bone, seemed to have an eating disorder. Another female guest had just discovered that she was pregnant, and hadn't told her boyfriend, who was also there, that she was. He meanwhile was making good headway with the alcohol addiction that eventually killed him. They were all very friendly to me, but they weren't my friends.

The villa was spectacular, built on a hill above the sea, and in the evening we gazed out from the terraces at the extraordinary Cycladean sunset staining the white houses pink as the flaming globe sank below the horizon, painting the dark sea red as it went. As soon as I arrived, though, it was obvious that my 'boyfriend' was no longer remotely interested in me. Many years later I learned that in the intervening weeks he had met another girl he had madly fallen for, but he hadn't had the heart or guts (I'm still not sure which) to dump me before the holiday.

Looking back at photographs of that holiday, one would never have been able to guess the cumulative misery of the group. There I was wearing tropical printed sarongs, gaily laughing during many long taverna lunches, and perched on a rocky beach in a tiny Provençal cotton bikini as we played backgammon, the men in mirrored sunglasses, denim jackets and chain-smoking Gauloises.

After a couple of weeks it was time to leave and I travelled with the pregnant girl on a ferry back to Athens. I dropped her at the apartment where she was staying for a night and went on to the airport, but when I got to the check-in desk I discovered that my ticket had been issued for the night before, not the date I had thought, and my plane had already left. An air-traffic controllers' strike had just been called and the airport was like a refugee centre, crammed with people trying desperately to leave. Because of the strike there was no alternative flight and anyway I couldn't have paid for one. I didn't own a credit card, and had spent the traveller's cheques we then used for the limited cash we could take out, and had only a couple of pounds worth of drachmas left. I spent the night sleeping on the floor of the airport loos, struck suddenly with the most incapacitating case of diarrhoea I have ever experienced. I was marooned in the city for days, dressed in the clothes I had chucked in a bag, stiff with salt and suntan lotion, until flights resumed and my parents, fortunately, paid for a new one.

About two weeks later I was in bed at my family's rented holiday house in Herefordshire when suddenly I couldn't breathe. My body was filled with what I now know to be a surge of adrenaline, but at the time felt like a poisonous, icy liquid rushing over me while a weight pushed down on my chest. I couldn't swallow. I thought I was going to die. It was the first of the panic attacks that have beleaguered me on and off throughout my life. I didn't realize that was what was happening and neither did anyone else in the house. None of us were acquainted with the term or symptoms of panic attacks. It was very many years before today's familiarity with mental health issues like anxiety and depression. Now I understand that first attack was linked to the terror I had felt when I was stuck at the airport, and which is liable to be repeated when I feel trapped in something I can't control.

For several years after that I very rarely travelled abroad. A combination of the fear of flying that took hold after that holiday and not earning much money meant I stayed put in Britain, often not taking all my allocated holiday. It wasn't that unusual for someone in their early 20s in those years, long before it became the norm to jump on a plane for a weekend festival in Slovenia or a wedding in Ibiza.

So my holiday wardrobe only began to be compiled many years later, when not only could I afford a holiday but I had a job that gave me something to be away from. When I left *Vogue* for a freelance existence, I quickly appreciated something I had never known about holidays, which is that they only exist in contrast to not being on holiday. To go on holiday means you have to return to something that demands daily application, probably doing things that you don't necessarily enjoy. Holidays are defined as much by what you are not doing as what you are. And so are our holiday wardrobes, those accumulations of treasured memories of delightful escape.

31.

Beanies

Intimations of mortality. The phrase comes to my mind as I make my way up the slope of the road to the cinema, where I am going to watch a film on a Friday afternoon. Why now? Maybe it's the cold weather, the slush that has pooled and is turning to an icy crush on the pavement and the darkening of the sky so early in the day. Maybe it's the fact that I have reached a stage in my life where I can go and watch an afternoon film – a wonderful indulgence but slightly sad. I no longer have people around me who expect me to be somewhere with them – an office, a child's teatime, handover from the nanny.

Intimations of mortality is a phrase I first read in a letter written to me when I was 17, by a man of 35 who used to write me pages and pages of cocaine- and alcohol-fuelled letters, typed on an IBM golf ball typewriter from the deck of a wooden house in Topanga Canyon, California. It's stuck in my head since then, and each time it comes to mind I think of the airmail stamp, the thin paper, the life he led so very far, in every way, from my own.

But here I am, no longer 17, and as I arrive at the Odeon Swiss Cottage in a grey wool beanie hat and a pair of spectacles, the guy at the ticket desk hands me a Senior ticket without my even asking. It is a low blow and follows dispiritingly on from the previous day when I was also wearing this hat and the same spectacles on the Tube. A young woman I worked with about three years ago sat down on the seat opposite me. At least I thought it was her, but I couldn't be absolutely sure. She looked about 20 per cent different to how I remembered her (more polished, glossier hair), but beside her there was an enormous black leather tote with the small gold lettering CELINE on it. Which was the final confirmation. She always loved an expensive accessory.

I stared at her hoping she would show a flicker of recognition that would allow me to greet her while not making a fool of myself in this crowded carriage by saying hello to a complete stranger. But she didn't. She looked directly at me, time and time again, but didn't see me. As I left the Tube I caught sight of myself in a reflection: an oldish woman in a grey hat and spectacles.

This is not the look that the many celebrities who wear similar hats as standard off-duty kit are aiming for – and neither was it, in all honesty, mine when I squashed it on my head. In Los Angeles, where January temperatures regularly reach the high 20s, Hollywood princelings are snapped holding reusable water bottles and smartphones while wearing beanies and short-sleeved T shirts. For both sexes the hat offers a smidgeon of hair-covering anonymity – but really only a smidgeon – but also a liberation from the endless demands of red carpet dressing and film costume. A woolly hat, denim, leather jacket – job done. Somebody who is of this world – the world of most people – but not quite.

Closer to home a beanie is an essential part of the school run, dash to the shops, not-in-front-of-the-cameras style of TV presenters and footballers. An item of clothing that is blindingly egalitarian but when worn by the rich and famous assumes a different identity. It's become an unlikely part of the uniform of celebrity.

The beanie is an interesting example of how fashion is driven by the people that we, as a collective, aspire to be. The theory goes that a certain look, trend or item is adopted by them, copied by us and then, when it might be threatening to become too common, the influencing group will move on in order to ensure that they do not merge with the hoi polloi. They need to make sure that they can be held apart and seen to be so, by adopting a different, newer style of appearance. In his 1930 book, *The Psychology of Clothes*, J C Flügel attributed the creation of what we would call fashion to this pattern. At that point he connected the influencing group to the class structure

– influencers then being higher up that traditional social pyramid, royalty and what would be thought of as nobility. But no longer, and not for decades. The birth of youth culture, street style and now the all-pervasive influence of social media are what position fashion today.

But despite the fact that on every Tube platform, service station checkout, football terrace and bus queue the single most common headgear is a woollen hat, it's still beloved by the famous of both sexes: Prince Harry and Meghan Markle, Hailey Baldwin and Justin Bieber, Adele, Ed Sheeran.

Beanies have travelled the distance. Fashion history has it that knitted caps were first worn for warmth by the hunters and fishermen of North America. With a tapered crown they are probably the closest ancestors to what we wear today. But another kind of knitted cap, flatter, thinner, was a staple of 16th-century clothing and in Britain the trade in knitted caps was so important to the economy that they merited their own act of parliament.

The 'Cappers Act' of 1571 stated that every person above the age of six years (except for 'Maids, Ladies, Gentlewomen, Noble Personages, and every Lord, Knight and Gentleman of 20 Marks Land') in England on Sundays and holidays should wear (except when travelling), 'a Cap of Wool knit, thicked and dressed in

England, made within this Realm, and only dressed and finished by some of the Trade of Cappers, upon pain to forfeit for every Day of not wearing three Shillings four Pence'. This act helped sustain the production of caps in England, thereby protecting a way of life for the many workers whose livelihood depended on them.

Personally, it's taken me many decades to wear a woolly hat out of choice. I needed first to recover from a variety of bad woolly hat experiences. From the age of seven a blue woollen hat complete with a long tail was part of my uniform at junior school. Kids from the local schools weren't saddled with such silly headgear, which marked us out as somehow different and not in a good way. And I still recall the uncomfortable business of having what we called a balaclava fastened under my chin years before that, as a very small child, for winter walks. The wool strap was rough and for the first few minutes of wearing felt like it would choke you, although I wouldn't have been able to describe it as such at three years old. It was simply not something I wanted to have put on me.

Balaclavas were named after the knits supplied for the British army in the Crimean War and the battle of that name. They included neck covering but not the menacing slits for eyes and lips of today's versions – the hideous black balaclavas worn in IS videos, the balaclava of the

Feeding the ducks in Hyde Park wearing my woolly hat, 1960

rapist, the ubiquitous balaclava of the intruder spotted in the juddering footage of CCTV spooled back for clues in a Netflix drama. But at root that threatening balaclava and the beanie hat of West Hollywood are not so distant. Anonymity is their shared purpose. Sure, the original item also shared the basic function of warmth, but that's not what an armed burglar or indeed Brad Pitt uses it for.

In February 2017, just days after 4.5 million people took part in the Women's Marches held in 700 cities around the world, I was sitting on a long bench in Milan waiting for the Missoni fashion show to begin. In each spot on the benches was a pink knitted hat with pussy ears in stripes of different shades of that colour. At the end of the show Angela Missoni urged the whole of the audience to join her, the models and the rest of her family, in a pink pussy-hatted moment on the catwalk as a gesture of solidarity with those marchers.

This was a particular time. The election of Donald Trump had lobbed a grenade into fashion's usual diplomatic lack of partisanship and during that A/W2017 season, just after his inauguration, everyone was talking about politics. This was, remember, six months before the #MeToo movement took hold. Before men in every industry were being called out for various kinds of abusive behaviour. Before women everywhere started to think it was worth mentioning that they had been groped by older, richer, more powerful men in the course of trying to build a career. It was a moment when putting on a pink beanie with silly ears seemed a fitting way of demonstrating that change was being demanded.

32.

Many Kinds of Black

Some of the reasons we like to wear black:

It makes us look slimmer
It doesn't show the dirt
It goes with everything
It looks serious
It looks chic
It's cool
It looks good with all skin colours
It looks good with all hair colours
It looks good

Except, basically, none of these are true. Or they are qualified truths. Or there's a little bit of truth, if truth can be quantified, but nothing that can stand much examination. However, that doesn't matter, since most of us still wear quite a lot of black. Black is all about who is wearing it, how and where.

Nora Ephron, that funny and perceptive chronicler of women's preoccupations, wrote the following about black in her book of essays *I Feel Bad About My Neck*:

Black looks great on older women with dark hair —
so great, in fact, that even younger women with dark
hair now wear black. Even blondes wear black. Even
women in LA wear black...Everything matches
black, especially black.

She's wrong about the last bit – more later. But she's right about LA.

I read her book just after having spent a few weeks there, and much of that time in the company of women who wore black. Exclusively. It seemed strange to me that they took this wholesale approach to a colour that went so spectacularly against the grain of everything that was fabulous about that city – the tropical display of palm trees, the brilliant azalea hedging, the strange emerald of the lawns, the cobalt blue of the sky (on days it wasn't muted by the marine layer). It's a city of intense colour, built on desert.

Nona is one of these women in black. She used to live in London and has spent many years battling addictions. Nona has thick curly auburn hair and now lives in a jewel of a house in West Hollywood that is filled with richly textured, patterned fabrics and earthy colours. I was curious as to her black clothes habit. She replied:

*'When I was a dysfunctional druggy I was far more
adventurous with colours. I feel safe in black. I feel
confident and since my hair/make-up and skin are
such a contrast there seems to be no need to wear any
other colour.'*

Although, she did conclude that,

*N.B. My three favourite coats are:
Vintage deep purple Ungaro couture, 1981
Lipstick pink YSL couture, 1978
Claude Montana lime green jacket*

The way these LA women wore their black was very
different to other city blacks of my acquaintance – New
York, Paris, London. It was mainly to do with things
other than the black itself. For example, their black
long-sleeved Ts, pants, sun visors, baseball caps and
of course sunglasses were a defiant protection against
the sunshine which both defines the city and also,
some think, creates a bland monotony. Black threw
into contrast their fragile, pale complexions – often the
result of many a cosmetic treatment and of having spent
at least the past three decades hiding from the sun in
an attempt to undo the damage of a youth basting in

coconut-scented Hawaiian Tropic around pools or on redwood decks or in an open-top convertible racing along the Pacific Coast Highway. And it came across as a demonstration of their seriousness and sense of purpose in a town so famous for the flickering of celebrity and the culture of youth. By the by – they almost all, to a woman, vote Democrat.

It's a very different look and feel to New York black, which is more like camouflage in that gritty, dirty, urban arena. As soon as you reach New York you feel like putting on some black. It makes sense. It's spare and efficient and doesn't waste space. Black seems to enable you to be the streamlined machine you need to be, capable of dealing with the intensity of a city where the jammed and towering architecture of central Manhattan allows you, only rarely, to catch a glimpse of a far horizon. So that everything is close up and crowds in. Donna Karan built an empire on New York black – calculating, rightly, that in black you could have a speedy 'pull it on, pull it off' wardrobe. She swathed herself in layers of it, as did her team. And even now, though fashion has moved on, there is something about the simplicity of a black pair of trousers, a black sweater, a black tote, that suits the place.

This in turn is not remotely the same as in Paris, where black is also a uniform of the city. Parisian black is insouciant, careless and all about the notion of a certain kind of chic, as much a part of the city as the tables outside the corner cafes and the gold dome of Les Invalides. A style typified by my former colleagues Carine Roitfeld and Emmanuelle Alt, both editors-in-chief of French *Vogue*, both models in their past life and both dressed a great deal of the time in black. Pencil skirts, jeans, leather jackets, pointed-toe ankle boots, strappy stilettos, blazers – all in perfectly tailored black but worn with a shrug. A black that carries the resonance of the Left Bank intellectual of years back, a black with the sexy hauteur of the work of Yves Saint Laurent. A black that is viewed as less pandering than colour, more 'take me as I am'. Even though, as we know, Parisian women and their black try just as hard, and possibly harder, than women everywhere else in the world to appear desirable.

Black came very late to the fashion milieu. It was rarely used until the mid-18th century, partly due to the difficulties of fixing dye which meant that black quickly faded to an unappealing, indeterminate grey. But as dyes improved and black became Queen Victoria's choice of colour for mourning, the wearing of that shade became increasingly popular in her Empire. Because so much of her long reign involved deep mourning, not only to be worn by her but by everyone at court, black gained a new prominence. Court dress was the fashion influencer of the day, with a trickle-down effect to the general public.

By the 20th century black had escaped mourning and become a colour women wore for work and pleasure, and also a colour that represented modernity. As Valerie Mendes quotes from a *Queen* magazine article of 1917, in her book *Black in Fashion*, '...the busy woman who has to take the metro, the tram or go on foot does well to indulge in one of the many little models in black'. Black was a part of the changed contemporary world.

The new fashion designers – now clothes were no longer run up only at home or by a local dressmaker – viewed black as sophisticated, treasuring its ability to demonstrate a purity of line and accentuate a silhouette. Cristóbal Balenciaga, Elsa Schiaparelli, Christian Dior, Coco Chanel, all favoured black. A practice which has continued through the graphic op art Sixties styles of Courrèges and Mary Quant, the seditious rebellion of punk, and the influential Japanese deconstructivists such as Rei Kawakubo and Yohji Yamamoto.

Do we consider this when we dress in black? Almost certainly not. I know I don't. I wear it usually for one of two quite contrasting reasons. First that I think it suits me, so in that I conform to Nora Ephron's reasoning. Most people think they suit black.

And sometimes I wear it because I wish to negate myself. Then it's into one of my old black T shirts, or one of my many black sweaters and a pair plucked from the thick forest of black trousers in my wardrobe that I can never tell apart. And that I buy again and again because I'm still searching for the ideal black trouser, even though I don't even know what that would be. It's not that I wish to feel negative at such times, but more to do with liking the idea of being only background, which is what black makes me feel. To not leave a footprint on the day.

Black is a negative – it is literally an absence of light, a negativity of colour. Alexander Theroux, in the literary magazine *Conjunctions 30*, described black 'as a colour, truculent, scary, deep and inaccessible…a bullying blot with a dangerous genius to it', which certainly gets the point over. It's why the density of black is so powerful and potent and why, in 2014, Surrey NanoSystems invented the densest black known – Vantablack – which traps 99.965 per cent of the spectrum, consequently containing only the barest smidgeon of light. So desirable was this that the artist Anish Kapoor licensed the spray paint Vantablack S-VIS for sole use by his studio, provoking outrage about the ownership of a shade.

The density issue is relevant to all of us because it's the reason why, in contrast to Nora Ephron's assertion, blacks really do not match easily, and blacks that don't match can look terrible. Black needs to be treated with care; weights and textures matter greatly. One black can throw off another, can make it look cheap and shoddy. And cheap-looking black has no allure, it is just a dark shade that you hope won't show the dirt. Black cotton will never look the same colour as black velvet. Nothing can look quite as sumptuous as black velvet.

I spent countless hours, weeks and months in the company of women in Fashion Industry black. It was particularly obvious during the fashion shows when the same cavalcade of buyers and press from across the world travelled to Milan, Paris, London and New York laden with suitcases of black clothes. The untutored eye might have imagined they wore the same thing every day, but that was of course not the case. They and I were in Calvin black, Prada black, Azzedine black, Jil (when Jil Sander was still in charge of the eponymous house and referred to that way) black, Balenciaga black...the roll call is long. The fashion shows were filled, row after row, with well-cut black coats and trousers, spindly high black heels and bare ankles. One autumn afternoon after a show I watched a trail of women with their slim legs in trousers, cropped jackets and precipitously high gladiator-style shoes, picking their way across the grass in Hyde Park like a breed of etiolated pterodactyls – all in black. To anyone who happened to stumble across it, it must have been the strangest sight.

Again, at the epicentre of the fashion business there was an Orwellian element to black – some black wearers were (and no doubt still are) more equal than others. While the editors and publishers of magazines, and fashion buyers of what at that point were the hugely wealthy and influential American department stores, would wear black, so too was it the uniform of the worker bees. The countless young men and women who manned the PR showrooms, who ushered us to our seats, who were the communications aides to the designers of the day, dressed almost always in a black trouser suit – maybe in summer in a shift.

My friend Fiona is someone who also wears black at least 80 per cent of the time. 'Black is who I am,' she says. 'I see myself in black and think, "That's who I am."' Who she is, when she is wearing black, is 'complete', 'sure', 'clear', 'chic'. Which by any terms is achieving a lot. But black really is the great all-rounder. It is extraordinary in being both a colour of power and also of servitude: the black uniform of sweatshirt and jeans worn by the girls in the local nail bar or the catering staff at parties; the professional black of the group of women I met the other day, gathered at a leading legal firm's breakfast to discuss issues of privacy; the obviously expensive and quite often confusingly elaborate black so often seen at art world opening parties. It can make us feel both invisible and, should we wish, highly visible. It was no accident that the Princess of Wales appeared at London's Serpentine Gallery gala in a plunging black cocktail dress the night her husband admitted his adultery on prime-time TV.

It may be no coincidence that, as black clothes gained in popularity, so did the existence of the physical clothing label come to prominence. It's hard to tell immediately whether a crowd in black are wearing Commes des Garçons or Zara. As more clothes were mass produced or made by a named designer, the label was introduced, stitched into a place that was relatively easy to find – like the inside neck. It was part of the recognition of how difficult it might be to produce a certification of the item's provenance and ultimately their worth. The slight problem of labels worn inside and consequently being known by the wearer alone has obviously been countered in the growth of logos spattered all over the place. But generally not over a discreetly elegant, black cashmere coat. Because elegant black, luscious black, confident black, can manage on its own.

33.

Tights

Our mother, in the tradition of the French kings, had something of a public levee. Her morning bath, rather than a private time, was often accompanied by us children, who sat on the little wooden chair with a plastic yellow seat opposite or explored the mystical contents of the bathroom cabinet while she bathed. And who would then follow her, me often with a trail of apprehension about the day ahead, into the bedroom where we sat on the bed to watch her dress. That was the time we could spend with her before she left for the office and the activities that took her away from us.

I remember a particular movement she would make during that daily ritual. She would stand in front of the mirror on the inside door of the fitted cupboards dressed in bra and a girdle, from which hung the suspenders to which she would attach her stockings. And having slowly eased each nylon up her leg she would clip a section of the fabric at the front and then twist her body around to clip the stocking on at the back, repeating it for each leg.

Stockings, then, to me, epitomized how it would be to be a woman. How it would be to dress as you wished, rather than either in a school uniform or in clothes that were chosen by someone else – dreaded tartan 'trews', as Mum called the baggy trousers she was fond of dressing us in, or pleated skirts and knee-high white socks. How it would be to have a day ahead filled with interesting things that your children knew nothing about. Stockings were rich with possibility.

Tights, on the other hand, were for children. They were usually of ribbed wool and the elastic at the waist often 'went', which meant you were frequently having to yank them back up to stop them hanging down uncomfortably between the legs.

Many of my friends also wore pale pink tights because they did ballet at school. An activity which, thankfully, did not include me, since my previous, bruising experience of a dance class was as a three-year-old who was allocated the role of thunderstorm when all the other little girls were raindrops. On special occasions we would also wear white lacy tights. They were scratchy but they were an essential part of dressing up for an event like a party where hopefully one was going to win prizes and get a going-home present.

The day eventually came when I graduated from these tights and was bought my own slim suspender belt and pair of tan stockings with a denser top. I stood like Mum in my bedroom and tried the whole kit on. Fortunately, this was a period when I had my own bedroom – the fluctuating bedroom arrangements in our flat meant a single bedroom allocation was always temporary. To have my younger sister mock me for my appearance at that moment would have been mortifying. And it would have been desperately annoying to hear her claim, as I suspected she would, that she should be allowed to skip the years I had put into getting to this point, the point where I could wear stockings, and that she should be allowed to wear them too.

The experience of wearing stockings was distinctly weird. The band cut into my belly, and feeling the clips press into the flesh of my thighs created a sensation around that area of the body which was unfamiliar and unsettling – it being a part of my anatomy that I had previously little to do with. But it was worth putting up with because it made me feel wonderfully adult.

Unfortunately for the 12-year-old who was longing for the sophistication I saw imbued in a suspender belt, I was coming too late to that particular party. No young woman worth their cred in 1969 was thrilled by the idea of stockings. Stockings were yesterday's news. Tights were the future.

Hosiery, a word which is hardly used at all and, when it is, is most likely to appear on the floor plan of a department store or on a website menu, has been part of our wardrobes for millennia. A pair of stockings was discovered as part of the hoard stored in an Egyptian noblewoman's tomb – it is interesting that they were a female possession because, as time passed, hose increasingly became associated with men rather than women.

We know that Chaucer's Wife of Bath wore 'hosen' of 'fine skarlet redde', but women's legs for centuries were hidden under long skirts, whereas men's legs were increasingly on display along with their hose – be that socks, stockings or tights. A fine leg was a manly compliment. Men would pad out their calves to get an idealized curve. As time passed more leg was on display, and hose were worn under thigh-length doublets.

'Men in tights' has become a catchall for male actors in historical dramas, but over the past century tights have become a leading accessory to gender-bending. Every Christmas our father would take us to the first night of the West End production of *Peter Pan*. The expedition was a much-anticipated highlight of our year, and Peter was always played by a girl, flying in through the open nursery window with an elfin crop, a tunic...and tights. It never seemed remotely curious to us that Peter was a girl – although admittedly this is a story where Nana, a large shaggy dog, is left *in loco parentis* as the Darling parents go out for the evening.

Peter is reassuringly sexless, even though he clearly falls for Wendy, provoking the wrath of his previous companion, the fairy Tinkerbell. He flies above the stage and darts around the set in a costume that is deliberately genderless. Could Peter Pan have been wearing trousers? I doubt it. Not on my watch at any rate. Could he have been an actual boy in tights, more like a ballet dancer with their pronounced genital area? Surely that would transform him into a far more dubious character, lording it around a tribe of young boys in Neverland.

Instead Peter and his tights were unthreateningly girlish. Much as many of my pre-adolescent love objects were, pop singers like Davy Jones of the Monkees and David Cassidy. Boys, for sure, but only a few notches of masculinity away from a girl. Not that they wore tights, unlike that other gender-mashed David, David Bowie, in his wildly sexual incarnations of Ziggy Stardust and Aladdin Sane. Or the 16-year-old boys we would hang out with in the Rainbow Room at Biba, who also wore eye make-up and lipstick and the same skinny satin scarves as us wound louchely around their necks. As Bowie observed in Mick Rock's *Glam! An Eyewitness Account*, 'I still derive immense pleasure from remembering how many hod-carrying brickies were encouraged to put on lurex tights and mince up and down the high street, having been assured by know-it-alls like me that a smidgen of blusher really attracted the birds.' Boys in tights had become overtly sexual just at the moment when, for women, tights represented the complete opposite.

Tights were part of women's liberation. They allowed women to wear their short skirts freed from the eroticism and inconvenience of a stocking top that could be exposed by any upskirting. We could climb up bus stairs, hop in and out of cars, wear them under hot pants. Stockings were eagerly exchanged for tights despite dire warnings of gynaecological health hazards, as demonstrated by an exchange of letters in the *British Medical Journal* over an increase of 'ladies' complaining of pruritus vulvae, a vaginal itch, under the heading 'Wearing Tights'. The solution, one medic suggested, was soaking tights in boracic acid after washing. Apart from that slight problem, the advantages of tights were on a par with the advent of the washing machine – they just made life a whole lot easier.

More than 40 years on and we're still wearing tights, though they remain uncomfortable and sweaty, confining (just like their name) and resolutely unattractive as objects in themselves. Despite a determined trawl to discover either a quotation or a film scene where tights were portrayed in a deliberately attractive light, I have failed. Whether you would consider the appearance of crotchless or ripped fishnet versions in porn clips as attractive is a matter of personal preference.

Some women, though, have a way with tights. Diane von Furstenberg is one of them. The last time we met was in her offices right by the High Line in New York. The building was filled with portraits of Diane, and her own office was a vast room housing books, sofas, massive tables, family photographs. She always displayed her long legs under short dresses, and on that occasion I remember them in patterned tights beneath what was essentially a loose shirt, as she bent over a large chest in her office, rummaging for a half-dollar coin, which she taped to the side of one of her brand's leather Scorpio wallets, presenting me with it for good luck as I embarked on the next chapter in my life.

She, the woman who brought us the wrap dress that became a signifier of liberated women, that was meant to be something we could slip quickly in and out of, that would both flatter and contain, should certainly know about tights. Bulky suspender belts and stocking tops played no role in her sensuous inventions. Diane wears tights like she wears her short dresses and her flaming mane of hair, as a defiant spirit.

When I arrived in her office that day I was feeling melancholy. It was snowing, a wet sloppy snow. I had

Diane von Furstenberg in 2014

been killing time in a burger bar on Tenth Avenue, and the famous guitar riff that kicks off the White Stripes' 'Seven Nation Army' played in a remix, again and again. And as I sat there I remembered my son, Sam, strumming those exact chords on a guitar ten years ago. Ten years? Twelve years? How long was it? Was he ten then? How old is he now? And I was overcome by how many years ago that was and how they were now gone. Impossible to retrieve. Suddenly I was aware of the incipient and insidious melancholy just under my skin which might so easily be triggered by leaving *Vogue*. Would I be at its mercy, unrooted and floundering?

When I left Diane's office I felt no such uncertainty. It might have been the silver coin or perhaps the ginger tea, and was almost certainly the exposure to her persuasive energy. But it was also helped by the experience of sitting across from a 70-year-old woman who was able to sprawl so very splendidly on a sofa, looking so great in her tights.

34.

Gold Dresses

The December 2000 *Vogue* was a gold-themed issue. Every page was filled with gold objects and gold typography, and the cover was Kate Moss's head in silhouette, hair piled up to show off her long slim neck, in profile against a glimmering deep gold base. In its unashamed opulence and shining glamour it appears from another age – which it was.

There were £3,000 gold leaf chairs, a gold ingot bag by leather maestro Bill Amberg, an £8,500 gold watch designed by Marc Newson, a recipe for Golden Risotto by Nigella Lawson, gold cocktails, gold bracelets and even a gold reindeer scattered throughout the pages. And, naturally, there were gold dresses. Many of them worn by the models of the moment: Leah Wood in vintage gold sequins, Tom Ford favourite Georgina Grenville in a Gucci silk jersey mini dress and Liberty Ross in a specially commissioned Hussein Chalayan gown.

I used gold often in *Vogue* as a shorthand for so many things: achievement, wealth, mythology, history. Of course, I was not alone in tapping into those associations. Gold is the most potent of materials, and when you consider the unassailed position of gold for so long in our society, it is really quite remarkable.

Gold's malleability, effectiveness as a conductor of heat, universally agreed beauty and relative rarity have always been strong arguments for its position at the pinnacle of worth, but even so the value of something only exists by a collective agreement. It is perfectly possible that gold could have been deemed worth not much more than tin. But from the earliest days gold was considered superior – the ancient Egyptians gave it a value of twice that of silver, and to this day an investment in gold is still regarded as one of the safest you can make. On a less practical level, gold continues to represent something positive, privileged and extraordinary: the golden days, the golden years, the golden hour, the tragic golden lads and girls of Shakespeare's *Cymbeline*.

It follows that dressing in gold is not something most people do on a daily basis – you find very little of it on the daily commute. Instead gold is reserved for special occasions. You kind of have to be in the mood to wear gold. You have to be ready to shimmer and sparkle. When the stars are in alignment it's a clothing colour that really can be empowering.

Be that the case, I have only ever owned two gold dresses. And both during the *Vogue* years. The first was designed for me by the London designer Emilia Wickstead when I was to host a party for the opening of the Westfield shopping centre in Shepherd's Bush. There's a kind of disconnect there – the idea of the gold dress and the pedestrian nature of the shopping mall, but that was what I chose to wear. To reach the festivities guests had to pick their way through a dark maze our production company had designed to disguise the reality of the situation, which was that they were only feet away from the less glamorous reality of a shopping centre. My dress was a gold shift, so pale it was almost white, lined in silk and, as it turned out, particularly useful since the party was held in very low lighting and the dress made it more likely I could be found.

My other gold number was for a very different spot on the party spectrum. In July 2015 David and I were collected at Genoa airport and chauffeured to a hotel on the Ligurian Coast, near the enchanting seaside harbour of Portofino. Portofino is where Italian designer Domenico Dolce had one of his homes and it was where he and his partner Stefano Gabbana decided to show that summer's Alta Moda (High Fashion) collection. These shows had become annual extravaganzas, events where the couple hosted a sumptuous Italian weekend for a few press and many clients who would then, it was hoped, order extraordinary and expensive pieces from this bespoke collection.

The outings were a real treat. Delicious dinners, time for ourselves to explore the various places they were held – Taormina, Capri, Venice – and a display of fashion at its most fantastical. That summer's show was inspired by *A Midsummer Night's Dream*, a play where the bucolic shenanigans were a perfect fit for the duo's rampant imagination. As the sun began to set the audience climbed a rocky path to a hilltop glade where boyish Pucks hung suspended from the trees, Renaissance pages held floral canopies over us guests and models paraded in theatrical gowns topped off with Titania crowns and angel wings.

The very existence of these shows was an indication of how, post the crash of 2008, the world of the very wealthy not only bounced back but expanded. Increasingly, many of the industry's most enthusiastic and extravagant clients came from new territories that had previously been seen as less important to the business but now fuelled its growth. Russia had obviously been in the frame for some time, as well as China and the Middle East, and clients from these regions were always part of the Alta Moda experience. But there were also characters like the Patagonian couple who owned the Honda car concession and who built their entire annual travel schedule around these parties, the entrepreneur who specialized in post-communist securities, and his Kazak bride and a Lancastrian widget manufacturer and his wife. These were people unlike those I spent my daily life with but who fascinated me with their enthusiasm for appearing wealthy. I was struck by the unfiltered pleasure they were taking in the money they had made.

The dress code for the Sunday evening gala dinner was gold. I and several others in our group who didn't have a gold party dress to hand imagined we could get away with wearing something else. But that was not to be. Stefano and Domenico wanted gold, and gold they would have. In the shops that lined the picturesque harbour they had a pop-up store selling items related to the Alta Moda – Portofino scarves and tote bags, iPhone holders and cotton skirts, all in the gay Fifties colours associated with holiday postcards. And rails of gold clothes. Simona, who worked with 'the boys', found me a long sleeveless sheath dress the colour of an antique Roman coin and flat jewelled gold sandals, and that evening we were all whisked by Riva speedboat to the party, where Kylie Minogue performed and the pair led the dancing in gold tuxedos. As they had wished, the evening glowed.

Light radiates from gold and reflects on the wearer flatteringly, which is why almost nobody looks bad in the colour. More symbolically, gold dresses are for winners, so

In Portofino wearing a Dolce & Gabbana gold dress, 2015

they were the obvious choice when British *Vogue* was asked to create the fashion segment for the closing ceremony of the 2012 Olympics. As always in such situations, we were given no budget by the organizers to shoot the huge images they wanted to use in the stadium. *Vogue* would have to finance the shoot. And of course we did.

We asked the photographer Nick Knight to work with us on this. Not only was he British (a qualification for this particular, patriotic job) but more importantly we knew we could rely upon him to create images that would have the visual power and punch needed to make an impact in the vast stadium.

Since it was to be a celebration of British talent we chose British models of the day – Georgia Jagger, Karen Elson, Stella Tennant, David Gandy, Lily Donaldson, Jourdan Dunn, Lily Cole, Kate Moss and Naomi Campbell – to appear in gold outfits designed for this occasion by a range of British designers. The deadline was very tight, and the designers had to drop everything to meet it. To complicate things further, the models had to be flown in from all corners of the world where they were working, not only for Nick's shoot but also to appear on stage on the evening the games closed. It was a logistical migraine.

There was a Mexican standoff when Kate and Naomi were equally determined to wear something by McQueen, whose creative director Sarah Burton said she only had time to make one outfit. I don't remember how this was resolved but in the end Sarah did manage to conjure up a second dress by the deadline. Stella Tennant was the odd girl out in a Christopher Kane glam-rock gold trouser suit that suited her androgynous appearance. The redheaded Lily Cole looked an intriguing Victorian sprite in gold Erdem lace and Jourdan Dunn was splendid in a Stephen Jones designed headdress, draped over David Gandy, the token male.

At the ceremony, huge billboards featuring Nick's pictures in black and white were wheeled onto the stage to the sounds of Bowie's 'Fashion', accompanied by a very peculiar marching band of gold-helmeted, oompa-loompa figures. The models followed, styled both for the shoot and the evening by Lucinda Chambers in a glittering, golden parade; Kate, with her unique ability to be coolly resplendent in a column of McQueen sequins, and Naomi, towering above the rest of them in her gold-dusted tulle cape and sequined platform wedges. It was a moment of untarnished gold.

35

Utility Wear – a.k.a. Boilersuits

I first saw Cathy one morning at the start of the term she arrived at my school to study for A levels. She was seated on a ledge in the wood-panelled library and, although she was new and wouldn't have known many pupils in her year, she was already the centre of a gang of girls. She had long, dirty blonde hair and the pale face of an angel. She was wearing a pair of oversized, blue and white striped OshKosh dungarees.

Beauty demands a slice of imperfection to lift it above the blandness of prettiness. Francis Bacon, the late 16th-century philosopher, put it this way: 'There is no excellent beauty that hath not some strangeness in the proportion.' Cathy, in her dungarees, with her broad face and wide-apart eyes, epitomized that in a way that has resonated with me for over 40 years.

Most of the women I find beautiful have a sliver of Cathy about them. She was not only to my eyes beautiful but terribly badly behaved, which only added to her allure. Think Marianne Faithfull as a fairly accurate comparison, in every way. Many of us at school wore those exact dungarees at that time but, where we bore a distinct resemblance to Andy Pandy, on Cathy they were undeniably sexy. It was something to do with the combination of this piece of sack-like clothing with her gaze of warped innocence.

I thought of her again the other day as I wandered around the stores filled, this season, with boilersuits. Hanging on endless rails and mannequins were boilersuits, boilersuits, boilersuits, with their zip fronts, long sleeves and patch pockets. Boilersuits in blue and black denim, grey cottons, khaki, creams; a more utility version of the jumpsuit and one step on from bib-front dungarees.

I very much wanted to buy one of these boilersuits for myself. This despite the fact that I am experienced enough to know that they have never looked good on me. Not even when I was young. Not even when I was slim. I don't have the right proportions. But that wasn't going to put me off trying. Deep down, I recognized that my yearning for a piece of clothing that I knew would not suit me was still, all these years – decades even – later, because I wanted to look like Cathy. And although most people, actually, I am sure *nobody*, buying a boilersuit today would have the faintest idea of what she looked like in her dungarees, I am certain that how she looked is really what they want to look like when they buy theirs. They want a piece of that determinedly unsexy sexiness.

Boilersuits are the great pretenders. You think that they disguise your shape but the opposite is true. If you have large breasts they are exaggerated, short legs are shrunk further by an all-in-one. And importantly it's the depth of the torso that is crucial, not the width. A body needs to hang around in a boilersuit, not fit snugly. And this bagginess then puts a huge demand on the few bits of flesh on display to be refined. Otherwise, on most people the look will be more Winston Churchill War Cabinet than they perhaps wished for.

Unlike most utility styles that evolve into fashion personalities, there is very little about the images of men wearing the original boilersuits – worn to maintain coal-fuelled boilers – that is remotely aspirational. Those one-pieces were designed specifically to keep the soot away from the skin while keeping the wearer's clothes on beneath. They were practical. Full stop. As were the wartime boilersuits that women wore. It's hard to imagine that any of those women would have thought there might be a time when they would climb into one, sling on a pair of strappy Jimmy Choos, pull the zip down to show off the swell of their breasts, roll up the sleeves and party on.

But at the start of the Seventies utility clothing gained a patina of style, and was taken up by the wealthy and urban and politically engaged. At least up to a point. A

Linda Ronstadt performing in a boilersuit, 1984

point skewered in Tom Wolfe's *New York Magazine* article 'Radical Chic: That Party at Lenny's', about an Upper East Side soirée hosted by the composer Leonard Bernstein. A party where the writers Mike Nichols and Lillian Hellman, the photographer Richard Avedon and film director Otto Preminger shared canapés with a group of Black Panthers, the revolutionary African-American movement of the age.

Radical Chic was born – not only a movement where fashionable revolutionaries dined with wealthy New Yorkers, but where the exotic wardrobe of flower power was infiltrated by blue-collar worker clothing. Clothes like dungarees, plaid shirts, khaki, Doc Martens, Mao collars. And when American *Vogue* introduced a food column called Soul Food, which included a recipe for Sweet Potato Pone.

Linda Ronstadt might have appeared on the cover of *Rolling Stone* in lace camiknickers, but she would perform in military boilersuits. Yves Saint Laurent, the designer creating the modern woman's wardrobe, repurposed the safari jacket, and its many pockets were designed to house essential survival kit for the pavements of Saint-Germain. The bovver boots of the late Sixties, as worn by all the terrifying skinhead girls who congregated at the Tube station every morning as I hovered on the platform, as far away as possible, on my way to school, morphed into the chunky lace-up boots we all found fashionable – and still do.

If you cared about feminism, racism, imperialism, this was your style, born at a time CNN recently called the 'golden age of terrorism'. Across the Western world there were demonstrations and marches fuelled by rage over the Vietnam War, while internationally newspapers were dominated by grainy black and white pictures of left-wing terrorist groups. Especially of women like the gun-toting heiress Patty Hearst held in the sway of the Symbionese Liberation Army or Ulrike Meinhof of the German Baader–Meinhof gang.

Yet this kind of political dressing has always been skin deep, if that. Politics and fashion have rarely been comfortable bedfellows. Often it is only many years later that it's possible to see how the clothes of an age have been affected by the politics of the time. Unlike actors, singers, artists and writers, most famous fashion designers have been unwilling to speak out about their political views.

Overt politics is an area where fashion, often considered as an art form, departs from the more activist behaviour of others in that category – film, theatre, literature, art. With the noticeable exception of Vivienne Westwood, who has always been impressively unafraid of speaking out, and at one point Katharine Hamnett, there are few well-known designers who appear comfortable with making any political message through their work. Consider the most famous designers of the past century and you will be hard pressed to find a political commentary from any of them – Giorgio Armani, Ralph Lauren, Karl Lagerfeld. Or even today's newer names, Victoria Beckham, Stella McCartney, Nicolas Ghesquiere, Virgil Abloh. Environmental concern, yes. But political statement, unlikely. Political allegiance is too divisive for the commercial business of fashion.

A few days after that recent shopping trip, the one where I failed to find a boilersuit that looked remotely decent on me, I was in a car with another woman driving home late after a wedding. She was wearing a pale pink Simone Rocha dress and had a pearl clasp in her hair. She was about my age and height, though definitely slimmer. We were talking about wanting to buy something new and she said she'd just found a wonderful silk boilersuit in Topshop. Naturally, this was irritating. Irritating, not because she had found one she liked, but because she should be able to wear a boilersuit that I had tried on, and wear it well, while I couldn't.

But there are some things you just have to accept in life, really. In the overall scheme of things, it is of course of no importance that I look terrible in a boilersuit and that she doesn't. But in the smaller scheme of things...well, that's a different matter.

36.

Dressing Gown

In the early autumn of 2016 I set off to the Suffolk town of Aldeburgh to move into a flat I had rented overlooking the North Sea. The car was filled with bedding, a stovetop coffee maker, my favourite bath essence, vodka, olive oil, yellow legal pads, a portable radio and two suitcases of clothes that I wanted to keep there for weekends, including a blue, green and yellow plaid brushed-cotton dressing gown.

I drove alone to set everything up before David arrived the next day, in an attempt to make it somewhere that would be appealing to him, who had rather less enthusiasm for this project than I. He felt no need to escape to a Victorian seaside town with a shingle beach, but I did. I had just finished the heavy lifting involved in *Vogue*'s 100th anniversary year: an exhibition at the National Portrait Gallery, a book, a fashion festival, a BBC television documentary, a gala dinner and a special centenary issue. After all this intense, demanding and also exhilarating activity, life seemed a bit flat, and I was searching for something different, although I had no idea what. I thought the Aldeburgh flat might be the answer.

I had plans to write poetry, paint bad watercolours, play the guitar and just be. To be me, in a place unconnected with my job. In a place that wasn't even mine so I would be free from much of the domestic responsibility of home – the cracks on the ceiling, the chipping paintwork, the never quite getting the sitting-room furniture right. On the first morning, I wrapped up in the dressing gown and made a pot of coffee on the small gas cooker, poured it into a Thermos and walked with it across the road onto the shingle beach, where I sat watching the sun rise above the sea. The gulls circled scraps of fish thrown out by fishermen, who were preparing to sell their fish for the day in the shacks that line the beach. It was glorious.

The dressing gown was a birthday present from my mother which I had asked for. It was from Toast and old-fashioned, in the style that predated central heating and was usually worn by men, possibly with a pair of sheepskin slippers, to shuffle down the stairs to breakfast. Large, with a long tie belt and deep pockets, it was as soft as a cloud but also protective. It's one of many dressing gowns that I have collected.

Dressing gowns are the transit lounges of life. You wear them as you wait to move from one state of being to another – from sleep to day, from bathing to dressing. In my opinion you can never have too many. There is one of bright, pale green towelling, trimmed with white tassels, which I bought in Istanbul's Grand Bazaar, a white cotton one with a colourful butterfly embroidered on the back that I was given years ago by the designer Matthew Williamson, another the result of a collaboration between a Provençal cotton and an Indian textile company that I rushed to buy in a shop just before a fashion show being held in Paris's Beaux-Arts. And there's the most recent addition to my collection, a dark blue and cream striped kimono in thick cotton provided in our hotel room on a recent trip to Luxor, which I asked if I could buy to bring home.

But it is the plaid one that concerns us here. I wore it to walk to the beach for freezing but invigorating morning swims in the icy sea and to scuttle back to the warm flat. Sometimes I wore it to cycle the short journey down the high street to buy the morning papers. It was what I reached for when I woke, pottering first into the kitchen with the portable radio and then into the sitting room, where I could spend hours studying the gulls nesting on the tiled roofs opposite and later bringing up their chicks before they learned to fly. I would watch them stand on the chimneys, all facing the same direction into the wind, to get lift for flight.

Aldeburgh was where I realized that what I was looking for was in fact a new life, and for that I must leave

Vogue. It was where one morning I woke up, watching those gulls preparing for flight, and realized that the future without *Vogue* was not the dark and frightening place I had previously thought but a bright, empty space ready to be filled with different adventures. I hoped that when I jumped, like those gulls, I would be facing the right direction for lift-off.

Three months after arriving in Aldeburgh I resigned and about six weeks after that, in late January, I was allowed to announce the news to my staff. I was terrified of that moment. It was like abandoning a family. It was, though, nearly four months more until Edward Enninful was announced as my successor.

By spring another dressing gown, in a thinner cotton with a blue and white African block print, had replaced the plaid for my Aldeburgh mornings. Both David and I loved the sharpness of the light there, the small life that we had playing tennis, dining in a rotation of three of the restaurants in town, reading for hours in the collapsed armchair and sofa in the sitting room and eating at the small round table in the window. I would think about how I would be able to spend weeks rather than weekends there once I left. Would I, though, know how to spend such free time? During one of the many conversations we had about my future, David asked me to consider how I valued free time. Would having nothing I had to do be something that would give me pleasure?

I realized with slight panic that I didn't recognize that notion. A few years earlier a friend had advised me not to give up my job without knowing what I was going to do afterwards. Four of his friends had done that, he said, and had all become alcoholics. When I order a glass of rosé at lunch at the local pub, his words come to mind.

At this time my dressing gown life was a delightful contrast to the mounting chaos around my departure. When I resigned to my boss Nicholas Coleridge he was silent for a couple of seconds and then he leaned back in his chair and said he was sorry I was going but he wasn't surprised. Jonathan Newhouse, the president of the company, was kind about my leaving but asked me to agree to stay at least six months so that they had time to find my replacement. If they hadn't managed by then would I be prepared to stay longer? I said I would.

In retrospect, it is clear that once my replacement had been announced I should have left. As things became more complicated I offered to, but I was told that I must stay until June as had been originally agreed. But that was becoming increasingly difficult. Traditionally, a new Editor-in-Chief can make no executive decisions until they are in the job, but Edward was being allowed to commission and hire and fire from a distance months before he arrived. He and I had had one meeting where I ran through who on the staff did what and talked a little about the working of the magazine, a meeting that was perfectly amicable, and I was unprepared for what was about to happen.

Shortly after it was announced that he was to be the next Editor, he fired my fashion director Lucinda Chambers, who had worked on the magazine for 30 years, and appointed and announced her successor despite the fact I was still supposed to be in charge. Models who were close to him and had been booked for my remaining issues began pulling out and the *on dit* was that he was suggesting they should wait until he arrived. A narrative was growing up around British *Vogue* being a place that was filled with 'posh white girls' that he would be getting rid of. It was deeply unpleasant not only for me but for my staff, who didn't know who they were working for and how long they would have their jobs. Many of them were the breadwinners in the family.

Meanwhile Edward, I gathered, felt that I was not supporting him while I was still in the chair. And that I tried to undermine him after I left. The seeds were sown for an acrimony that I could never have imagined occurring after having worked for the magazine for 25 years.

In June I finally left *Vogue* and spent the summer swirling in the euphoria of freedom – from routine, from responsibility, from the horrible fallout from my departure and from getting dressed for the office. I spent much of that time in a dressing gown – taking conscious pleasure in not having to be dressed. I decanted boxes from *Vogue* into the office I was making myself at home. I started working on a proposal for a TV series. I began to consider this book.

Just before I left the magazine Elizabeth Saltzman, stylist to many celebrities, had told me that a danger of freelance life is that you might never get out of your pyjamas. She insisted that it was vital to avoid this. You MUST get dressed, she emphasized, along with giving me the number of a freelance IT guy. But at that point – in my case for pyjamas read dressing gown – being able to hang around in this pre-dressed state was a cause for celebration. It didn't mean that I had nothing to do, nowhere to go, I was indulging in it simply because for the first time in my adult life I could. Curiously, the one thing I had forgotten to pack when we left the Aldeburgh flat was that plaid dressing gown.

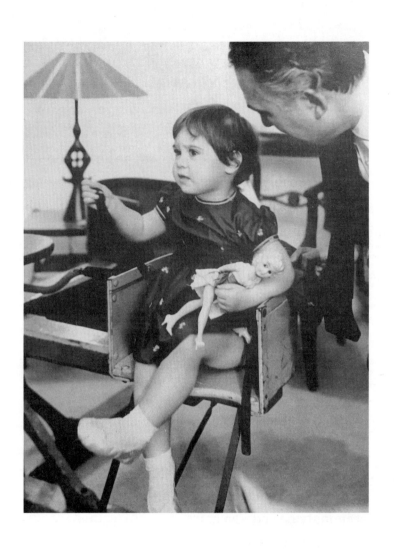

With my father, wearing my navy party dress, 1959

37.

Navy

Have you ever seen a teenager choosing to dress in navy? Probably not. Navy is like one of those people who were born, not middle-aged, not old, but simply never young, travelling through life in their own slipstream, unaffected by their peers. For this reason navy is the most reassuring of colours. It knows itself. It's not going to surprise or ambush you, and is safe in the best way possible. Or at least I have always found it to be so, and as a result I wear it. A lot.

Navy is my default when, really, I don't want to wear anything at all. When remaining asleep, unaware of the day ahead, is the most preferable option. On those days when it would be so much easier to let the world go about its business without you and the tangle of problems in your mind, each with an identifiable beginning but seemingly no end. On days like this, navy is kind. It's the St Christopher of clothing, infallibly helpful in carrying us through.

In spectacular fashion photographs navy is scarcely ever to be found. More often than not, though, it will be central to a Basics story, where a pair of navy trousers will be paired with a white shirt or very likely a Breton-stripe T. Unsurprisingly, but somewhat unimaginatively, it's also relentlessly styled with nautical touches – perhaps the trousers will be wide-legged sailor pants or there will be a jaunty cap involved or there will be a boat of some kind somewhere. Maybe an anchor. It's produced as a staple much in the manner of a breakfast cereal – a reliable pillar of your wardrobe. It is also a trusty component of Ageless Style stories. Navy may well rarely be the colour of choice for young people but ageless, when you boil it down, is usually a euphemism for no longer young, so that doesn't matter.

Actually ageless, when it comes to fashion, is confounding, since implicit in it is the very idea of age. If clothes are described as utility chic or boho or power dressing, age is irrelevant. But ageless chic? We know what that is about. It's about how you can still look passable once you reach an age where if you attempt a neon pink tulle meringue you will simply look like a freak. Although it's remarkable how many elderly women who adopt wildly over-the-top freak fashion are thought of as possessing great style. It's as if by wearing the seemingly unwearable at 80-plus you inhabit a whole other ecosystem where the odder you look, the more stylish you are considered to be.

That behaviour, though, has nothing to do with navy, which is not about looking odd. That's the very opposite of navy. Perhaps my personal fondness stems from when my favourite, absolutely best, dress was navy. I wore it for my second birthday party. The navy poplin fabric was decorated with occasional pale pink embroidered roses and it had pale pink piping at the neck and on the slightly gathered short sleeves.

Even that young, I was aware that this dark blue was different to the colour that most of my friends and I usually wore for parties. That would have been a pale pink or blue or yellow, or often white, just like my other best dress, which was white and trimmed with ribbons of scarlet silk that one day bled horribly from the wooden washing line that hung above our bath and could never be worn again.

After that my life was a navy-free zone. No doubt the reason most teenagers don't love navy is that it is so often a part of a school uniform and therefore something to escape from as soon as humanly possible. And because at senior school we didn't have a uniform, during that period it had no place in my life, and it played no part in the hippy, glam rock, proto-punk fashions that I followed either (well, the latter was only really a bit of fluoro and fishnets – no safety pins or bin bags for me).

Alexa Chung in a plain navy sweater, New York, 2013

But when I got a job on the *Sunday Telegraph* in the mid-Eighties, I bought a navy suit from Joseph with a short, straight skirt and a slightly waisted jacket, in order to have something professional looking to wear to work and also to have something new from Joseph, which in itself demonstrated membership of a chic urban tribe. Somebody who knew that when you went to Joe's Café in South Kensington, the fishcakes were the thing to order. That was the first navy jacket of the many I have owned since.

One of the defining qualities of navy is that it is not black. Although it shares a similar foil-like quality, a backdrop to the person wearing it, there is none of the drama of black in navy. Navy is an aide, rather than the star. The late Anna Harvey, a woman of immaculate taste and honour who was my deputy editor on *Vogue* for many years, rarely started or finished a sentence without including an apology. The apology, of course, was always completely unnecessary. She was brilliant in so many ways. She wore a lot of navy.

Those I think of as Lucian Freud women all wear navy too. The artist was often attracted to women of a particular type, with an intriguing fragility, pale skin and indeterminately coloured, unstyled hair. It was as if the appearance of these women, void of anything ostentatious or overt, allowed him access to a greater degree of exposure when he painted them nude. If you ever met such women they were often found in navy skirts, crew necks, mannish overcoats and flat shoes. Not a million miles away from school uniform. You won't find a Freud woman in hot pink.

It's the same quality shared by Jane Birkin who, with her straggly hair and small-breasted tomboy figure, made dressing in blue jeans and a shirt an art form. She is often photographed in navy. And at times Alexa Chung, who even when she is wearing an elaborate gala gown manages to strip it down to something that is metaphorically barefoot, and whose go-to is a navy crew neck sweater.

This plainness is ideal when you want to be indeterminate. When you don't want your appearance to lead to any conclusions. After I announced that I was leaving *Vogue* a friend offered me a complimentary session at an executive coaching partnership which gives advice to business leaders. I jumped at it, intrigued by what they might say.

As it happened, the meeting took place the day after my successor at *Vogue* had been announced, a day which had been more emotionally difficult than I had imagined it would be. My diary of 11 April 2017 reads:

Lots of people had said it must be difficult for me and it was, but I couldn't work out why. After all I had resigned. Somebody was always going to have to take my place. But it is a small death I suppose, and by this evening I have worked out that resigning was a step into the future but that this moment is the true beginning of the end of me and Vogue. I got such complimentary coverage when I announced my departure – but I realize now that the new King is announced this will be an opportunity for the snipers to line up.

I dressed in a navy cardigan and one of my many navy wool coats for the meeting, hoping to appear professional and not too much of a fashion cliché, and drove into Mayfair for the 7.30am appointment at their offices, which resembled my image of how an upmarket MI6 safe house would look – magnolia walls hung with prints, glass coffee table, grey sofas. There was no sound from the street outside. No clues to the personalities of the people who worked there.

Two men sat opposite me, probing as I perched on one of the grey couches, startlingly inquisitorial as they asked me about the new Editor and how I felt about leaving. They told me that having spent 25 years in one role I would have become institutionalized. That I would have no idea of how I appear to people who meet me outside of the context of *Vogue*. They warned that my greatest danger was that I had been doing the same job for so long that I wouldn't have the foggiest how to behave once outside it – or words to that effect.

'What will you say if you are asked to comment in the press about leaving?' one asked, glaring at me. I replied that I would say I was excited to be moving on and pleased that a new Editor had been announced. 'No. You will not,' he boomed. 'You will say nothing. And if you do say anything at all, it must not be negative.' I hadn't imagined that reply at all negative, but if I have learned anything much in the years between then and now, I have learned that they were right: a) that saying nothing is certainly the safest tactic, b) that anything I do say runs a good chance of being interpreted as negative and c) that I am not capable of keeping silent.

I leave their office fizzing with the prospect of terrible pitfalls awaiting me but grateful for their advice. A few weeks later they ask me to fill out a questionnaire as part of the Hogan Psychometric Assessments. It would, they suggested, give me some helpful ideas about what next steps I might want to take in my life.

When the results come back with an assessment of my strengths and weaknesses, they report they have discovered that I enjoy working in a team, need the approbation of other people and care what my working environment looks like. I find this rather fascinating. But that evening when I excitedly tell David their findings he says he can't understand why I consider that information illuminating. It just proves that the job I am best suited for is the job I have done for the past 25 years and had chosen to give up. He had always said that was a silly thing to do.

That was nearly three years ago, and in the intervening period I have worn just as much navy as before. It remains the colour I am drawn to when I feel vulnerable or when I want a little bit of support. I currently have 26 items of navy clothing in my wardrobe – not counting underwear.

Carl Erickson, American Vogue, *December 1943*

38.

Jewellery

One morning I was sitting at my dressing table, staring into its oval mirror. I have always loved a dressing table and was delighted when I came across this one in a local junk shop a couple of years ago. Dressing tables are so civilized, even one like this, slightly rickety with a broken leg strut. But dressing table or no, that morning I had a hangover. Why, I asked myself, as I have more often than I would wish, did it seem like a good idea to have the last two glasses the previous evening? Naturally, at the time it seemed like a tremendous idea. But last night, this morning was a lifetime away.

A new day has dawned and it is one on which I have shortly to meet a man who is interested in my doing some work with him, and also one on which I am being filmed for a short television interview about an exhibition. The person facing me in the mirror will not do. I have to make myself at least appear like somebody who is functioning effectively.

The thought of attempting to put together an outfit matching something with something else makes the hangover even worse, just as the coffee I have drunk has done. I am wearing a very plain navy dress which I decide, with the television interview ahead, looks too drab. So I turn to a necklace to add a bright and glowing element to the distinctly unbright, unglowing person I feel right now. And up to a point the necklace does achieve something of that. At least I think it does.

Jewellery is eminently helpful when it comes to adding a veneer of style and accomplishment. Which was one of the reasons why when I was invited to choose a print from the magazine archives as a parting gift, I chose one featuring jewellery. There were literally thousands of fashion photographs I might have picked, but after much toing and froing I decided that I would instead love a copy of an illustration from a 1943 edition of American *Vogue*. Drawn by Carl Erickson, a favourite *Vogue* illustrator of the period, it depicts a woman getting ready for what I have always assumed to be the evening ahead of her. The image, drawn in pastels and ink, represented the traditional glamour, elegance and escapism I always associated with *Vogue*.

The illustration shows a woman's head from behind, her hair swept up to draw attention to a double strand of large pearls fastened around her neck with a clasp. We can't see her face, but her nails are carmine-tipped and she is clipping on an earring that we also can't see and are left to imagine. What might it be? A diamond drop? She looks the diamond type and has another diamond, enormous and cabochon cut, on her wedding finger. It's a wonderful period piece and in the magazine was captioned, 'Give her pearls...not just an anonymous little strand that she might fasten on automatically...but great big ones like these.'

We are meant to think this woman leads a glamorous existence: it's demonstrated by the fashionable neckline of her violet evening dress and her classic jewellery – intended to show her good taste, position, elegance – the fine things in life. As evidenced by the caption, it is likely that she has not bought the jewels for herself. But it's 1943 and things were different then. This woman is perfectly happy with that. Being given jewellery will be considered its own mark of some kind of success. Her jewellery is a statement about who she wants us to think she is.

And that's the thing. Little of what we wear has the same sweep as jewellery. It's one of the most efficient multitaskers – trophy, love token, bribe, indicator of status, investment, good-luck amulet, heirloom. Despite the multitude of extraordinary changes that have taken place in almost every area of life, jewellery is still used for pretty well the same purposes as it has always been.

Primitive man is said to have worn a kind of ornamentation to enhance his sexual attraction as well as provide protection against all manner of disasters, from snakes to evil spirits. Cleopatra used jewels (with a particular fondness for emeralds) to seduce admirers and rivals not only on her body but in her home. They showed off her fabulous wealth and position. Julius Caesar ruled that only the highest born women could wear pearls, which were Rome's most valued jewels. Not only does our jewellery mean something to each of us, but it also has meaning to those who view us. Jewellery has forever been a currency understood by all.

Most of us have a collection of some kind of jewellery or another. There probably isn't much there worth a great deal in financial terms, but that's not the point. There will be a few studs and hoops for our ears, bracelets that we have gathered over the years, bits and pieces of broken metals and coloured stones on chains that at some point we intend to get fixed. And the odd piece that means something to us – something very much more than simply adornment or material wealth – perhaps a tangible marker of an occasion or a sentimental legacy. Often the items that are most painful to lose are those we have inherited – a grandmother's brooch, our mother's watch, our engagement ring. They are links in our personal timeline of memories and associations that make us the person we are. They are the ones that are particularly brutal to have stolen in a break-in, when they are of little worth to the thief and tremendous emotional worth to us.

My own collection of jewellery, while neither large nor extremely valuable, is filled with scraps of history. I have several boxes of tat sitting on the dressing table which have only nostalgic value. Most of them I haven't worn in years but even I can't contemplate giving them away, such as a blue and white glass Greek bracelet and a nickel teddy bear on a chain. There are other pieces given to me by men, pieces that at the time meant an enormous amount to me, and now so much less than I might ever have imagined they would: a slim string of jet beads, an ancient small jade owl hanging from a chain of antique garnets, a pair of Art Deco-style green stone earrings

But there are also the cheap bracelets which I am never without and have worn for over 40 years on my left wrist: a flat plait of Navajo silver and a cheap Indian band with some weird mythological animal head at its tips. There was also, until I lost it in a makeshift changing room in Camden Market, another bracelet that I always wore, a silver snake that my maternal grandfather gave me. He was blind, and I liked to imagine that he felt the scales and the shape of the head.

Why do I wear those other two? Not because I like how they look. Not because I any longer care about who gave them to me. But because they have become lucky talismans that are almost a part of my body. I don't even notice they are there, except for when I have to go through airport security and they frequently trigger the alarm.

And then there are the real stars. The square ring with a miniature square diamond that my godmother Toni gave me and which I always wear on the little finger of my left hand. Toni was married to a South African diamond tycoon and long after their divorce she split a necklace he had given her into individual stones and gave one of these rings to each of her goddaughters.

There is also the gold and topaz necklace my father gave my mother on the occasion of my birth: a delicate filigree web holding a dozen, faintly rose-tinted topaz, my birthstone. When my son was born, my mother passed that necklace in its original satin-lined black leather case on to me and probably, if the time should arrive, I will hand it on to a woman close to him.

More recently I have a faded pale jade velvet box in which a diamond and platinum necklace from Nikolai Linden, a St Petersburg jeweller, nestles, a present from my sister Nicky for my 60th birthday. The Russian provenance was a nod towards our grandmother Ethel, born there before leaving for a new life in Canada. Linden's store was on Nevsky Prospect and he was known for working alongside the much more famous Fabergé and also as a jeweller to the splendid-sounding Shah of Persia, the princes of Montenegro and Bulgaria, and the King of Romania. It's the piece of most obvious historical interest that I own.

Finally, there are the slender drop earrings I was given as a generous leaving gift from *Vogue*. They were commissioned for me from Californian jeweller Susan Foster in 18-karat yellow and white gold, green tourmaline and diamonds, something called cushion-cut champagne natural zircon, and touchingly have a capital A in fine gold on the back of each, in my handwriting. They carry no memories or history with them. They were a good luck token for the future. They are simply beautiful, luxurious, elegant and unique, all the things that I associate with the magazine that took up such a large part of my life. Qualities which that Carl Erickson picture hanging on my wall continues to conjure up.

Bibliography

In the process of writing *Clothes... and other things that matter* I have referred to the work of other writers. Where I have quoted directly the attributions are in the main body of the text but there are also writings listed here that I would like to mention that gave me inspiration or I enjoyed:

'Black', Alexander Theroux, *Paper Airplane*, Conjunctions:30, Spring 1998

Black in Fashion, Valerie Mendes, V&A Publications, 1999

Black in Fashion: Mourning to Night, National Gallery of Victoria, 2008

Clothing: A Global History, Robert Ross, Polity, 2008

Costume and Fashion: A Concise History (Fifth Edition), James Laver, Amy de la Haye and Andrew Tucker, Thames & Hudson, 2012

Dress and Globalisation, Margaret Maynard, Manchester University Press, 2004

Dressed: The Secret Life of Clothes, Shahidha Bari, Jonathan Cape, 2019

Floury Fingers, Cecilia H Hinde, Faber & Faber

Glam! An Eyewitness Account, Mick Rock, Omnibus Press, 2013

History of Hosiery: From the Piloi of Ancient Greece to the Nylons of Modern America, Milton N Grass, Fairchild Publications, 1955

How to Read a Dress: A Guide to Changing Fashion from the 16th to the 20th Century, Lydia Edwards, Bloomsbury Visual Arts, 2017

I Feel Bad About My Neck: And Other Thoughts On Being A Woman, Nora Ephron, Doubleday, 2006

Indigo: Egyptian Mummies to Blue Jeans, Jenny Balfour-Paul, British Museum Press, 2011

Jackie Style, Pamela Clarke Keogh, Aurum Press Ltd, 2001

Jeans: A Cultural History of an American Icon, James Sullivan, Gotham Books, 2006

Lady Behave: A Guide to Modern Manners, Anne Edwards and Drusilla Beyfus, Cassell & Company Ltd, 1957

'My Life as a Girl', Stephanie Burt, *The Virginia Quarterly Review*, 88(4), 2012

'"None but *Abigails* appeared in white aprons": The Apron as an Elite Garment in Eighteenth-Century England', Elizabeth Spencer, *Textile History*, 49(2), 2018

'Radical Chic: That party at Lenny's', Tom Wolfe, *New York Magazine, June 1970*

Read my Pins: Stories from a Diplomat's Jewel Box, Madeleine Albright, HarperCollins, 2009

'Snow', Louis MacNeice, *Collected Poems*, Faber & Faber, 2007

The Art of Dress: Clothes and Society 1500–1914, Jane Ashelford, The National Trust, 1996

The Blessing, Nancy Mitford, Hamish Hamilton, 1951

The Female Eunuch, Germaine Greer, MacGibbon & Kee Ltd, 1970

The Language of Clothes – Alison Lurie, Hamlyn, 1983

The Psychology of Clothes, J C Flügel, Hogarth Press, 1930

The Secret Lives of Colour, Kassia St Clair, John Murray, 2016

The Thoughtful Dresser, Linda Grant, Virago, 2009

The White Album, Joan Didion, Weidenfeld & Nicolson, 1979

This is not Fashion: Streetwear Past, Present and Future, King Adz and Wilma Stone, Thames and Hudson, 2018

Vogue on: Hubert de Givenchy, Drusilla Beyfus, Quadrille, 2013

Vogue on: Coco Chanel, Bronwyn Cosgrave, Quadrille, 2012

Vogue Essentials: The Little Black Dress, Chloe Fox, Conran Octopus, 2018

'What's Wrong with Cinderella?', Peggy Orenstein, *The New York Times Magazine*, December 2006

Women in Clothes, Sheila Heti, Heidi Julavits, Leanne Shapton & 639 Others, Particular Books, 2014

20th Century Fashion, Valerie Mendes and Amy de la Hay, Thames & Hudson, 1999

Index

Page numbers in *italics* indicate illustration captions.

Picture Credits

16 Pictorial Press/Alamy Stock Photo; 34 PAINTING/Alamy
Stock Photo; 59 © Telegraph Media Group Limited 2020; 94 World
Northal/Everett Collection/Alamy Stock Photo; 107 Horst P.
Horst/Condé Nast via Getty Images; 110 Oberto Gili/Vogue; 112
Courtesy of Sony Music Entertainment. Patti Smith, 1975 © Robert
Mapplethorpe Foundation. Used by permission; 120 The Jewish
Museum/Art Resource/Scala © The Pollock-Krasner Foundation /
ARS, New York and DACS, London 2020; 128 PA Photos/TopFoto;
140 © Tate; 145 © Kim Knott; 150 Philip Berryman/Vogue; 156
François Nel/Getty Images for Fenty Beauty; 162 Josh Olins/Vogue
© The Condé Nast Publications Ltd; 170 Dennis Stone/Shutterstock;
176 Photo: Maria Pavliuk; 187 Estrop/Getty Images; 189 © Liza
Cowan 1975; 190 Pigi Cipelli/Archivio Pigi Cipelli/Mondadori
via Getty Images; 207 Yavuz Alatan/AFP via Getty Images; 214
Image courtesy of The Advertising Archives; 230 Solo Syndication/
dmg media; 237 David M. Benett/Getty Images for The Business of
Fashion/The London EDITION; 244 Philip Berryman/Vogue; 252
Christian Vierig/Getty Images; 296 Bryan Bedder/Getty Images
for American Express; 310 Tim Mosenfelder/ImageDirect/Getty
Images; 326 © Elder Ordonez/INSTAR Images; 332 Carl Oscar
August Erickson/Condé Nast via Getty Images.

All other photographs are courtesy of the author.

Acknowledgements

I would like to thank everyone who played a part in the creation of this book particularly my mother Drusilla who encouraged me right from the start and inspired so much of what is written about here. I am hugely grateful to my agent Eugenie Furniss at 42mp who was a supporter and shaper of the original idea and as always spurred me on throughout. My publisher Alison Starling at Octopus has shown unflagging enthusiasm and understanding and creative director Jonathan Christie endless patience. Also thanks to Ella Parsons for her invaluable input and Giulia Hetherington for work with the images.

Louise Chunn was a truly helpful reader of the manuscript at a crucial stage and David Jenkins had the thankless task of being constantly asked for his opinion and then having to deal with my response. My gratitude for his being my wailing wall is endless.